BACK TO FRENCH LICK

A Memoir

Eva Sharron Kobee

authorHOUSE®

AuthorHouse™
1663 Liberty Drive
Bloomington, IN 47403
www.authorhouse.com
Phone: 1 (800) 839-8640

Published by AuthorHouse 11/26/2019

ISBN: 978-1-7283-2698-6 (sc)
ISBN: 978-1-7283-2697-9 (e)

Library of Congress Control Number: 2019913872

Print information available on the last page.

This book is printed on acid-free paper.

Contents

Acknowledgments

I cannot possibly name all who have helped me with this, my first book, but it truly would never have come about were it not for my wonderful family who gave me the courage to step out into unknown waters.

Thank you to my son, John Michael, for all of the hands-on, time-consuming, reading and re-reading of my ever changing manuscript. Your confidence in me made me believe in myself.

To my son Jeff, thank you for seeing the risk and romance in your parents' lives. You have helped me to see remarkable things that I had never before considered remarkable.

To my daughter Julie, thank you for being my "boots on the ground" in French Lick, researching and promoting, for trying to improve my grammar (but to no avail) and for your positive words that have reassured me when I wavered in faith.

To all of my children and grandchildren, your interest in our family's stories have encouraged me to recall many memories and to see them in a brand new light. You are a constant source of joy and adventure.

And to my great-grandchildren, you continue to affirm that the decisions of 1958 were most definitely the right ones.

But above all, I praise God from whom all my blessings flow.

In loving memory of my mother,
Wava Bertran Charnes McDonald,
the hand that rocked my cradle…

Introduction

When I finally decided it was time for me to write this book, I wasn't sure how to go about it. Eventually the words of my typing teacher in high school came back to me. She had said, "If you set a monkey in front of a typewriter long enough he will eventually type a word". So I figured that if I sat in front of my computer long enough I could eventually write a book.

My 'plan', and I did have one, sort of, was to write a book about the history of the hotel: all I had to do was dig up the information that I had used on my history tours and put them in a book; this would be simple.

For the history of the hotel that I did not remember or that simply was before my time, I found the thesis written by Richard Haupt in 1953 for the Master of Arts degree from Indiana University to be very informative. Mr. Haupt had interviewed many workers at the hotel whom I had known and respected, including my father, Frank McDonald, therefore giving me confidence in their accounts of the hotel's history.

I also found the book by James Philip Fadely, *THOMAS TAGGART, Public Servant, Political Boss, 1856-1929* to be very helpful in filling in and confirming the knowledge that I already had of the Taggart family.

Much information was also discovered in various old newspapers clippings and other papers I found stored in filing cabinets in the hotel when I first started working on a history tour of the hotel in 2000. I have tried to approach these sources with an eye for accuracy, comparing different accounts, trying to separate the National-Enquirer type "facts" from reality, because truth is often stranger and more interesting than fiction.

But as I began to write the hotel's history, my personal memories of growing up in the little town in southern Indiana with the curious name of *French Lick* kept jumping onto the pages.

These memories did the same thing when I would be giving a history tour of the hotel. I might be talking about the hotel being self-sufficient and growing its own vegetables and suddenly I would remember my father taking me to one of the hotel's gardens situated high on the hill behind the hotel, pulling a turnip out of the ground, wiping the fresh earth off of the turnip on his pant leg and using his pocket knife to cut off the top and peeling, then giving me a slice of the turnip to eat. These recollections were so persistently trying to get on the pages that there just wasn't anything I could do but let them have their way.

But memories and history were not all that came to light; I began to see truths that were mere shadows to me when I was growing up. As I began to look at my memories through the candlelight of time, I admittedly saw some of the past in a soft gloaming that muted many flaws. However, now that I was not being blinded by the harsh glare of reality that had surrounded me, I began to see a clearer, sharper view of my family and the culture that formed my values and ideas about life.

If the history and recollections that I present of the hotel at French Lick and the town of French Lick are in anyway contrary to others' memories and research, please remember that even eyewitnesses rarely agree on what they have seen. I am just looking through my eyes alone at a time that I remember and a time that I discovered.

Prologue

The last full moon of the 20th century had occurred on December 22^{nd,} Johnny's birthday. Orion, my favorite constellation, was rising over the apartment building on my right. Every time I saw the belt of that great hunter I would think about seeing him in the winter sky from my front porch when I was a teenager. He continued to remind me that even though I was miles and years away from that place and time where I became me, I *was* still *me*.

There was no snow on the ground this night, just frozen weeds, so walking wasn't as hard as it had been many times these past ten winters as I made my way to and from work, sometimes braving a snowstorm.

But this night I wasn't thinking about snow or cold; I was thinking that this was the last time I would ever walk through this field. I was thinking about all the people I had just said, "Goodbye" to and would never see again. Tears of sadness were falling from my eyes.

As I got closer to our apartment building I saw the silhouette of a large moving van. It wasn't unusual to see someone moving in or out of our complex, but this van was right in front of our apartment. That is when I realized that our son, Jeff and his son, Zach, had arrived and they were loading *our* stuff into this van.

I heard myself say, out loud, out there all alone, *"Finally, it's MY turn, I am really GOING HOME!"* And my tears turned from sadness to joy.

That night I was taking the first steps into the future that had been my heart's desire for so many years, little knowing that I would also be returning to the past that I had stored away in my memory…. and to a past I had never seen.

Chapter 1

Entering A New Millennium

December 31, 1999

We decided that if we were going to move in 2000, we might as well start
the New Year and the New Century out right. So January 1 was the target
date to begin our New Life.

January 1, 2000, was being viewed as a day of uncertainty, a day of dread,
a day for which to prepare. No one was sure what the first day of the new
millennium would do to life as we knew it. We started to hear over and
over the term "Y2K" as television, radio, and newspapers told everyone to
begin preparing for the approaching possible "day of doom". What made
this century different from all previous new centuries was the computer.
Would computers "think" those last two zeros signaled the year 1900?
Would there be no electricity? Would we be unable to buy food and other
necessities if scanners and cash registers became incapacitated? Would gas
pumps stop working? Would banks fail? So we tried to be responsible and
make sure we had some basic necessities, "just in case": extra batteries,
portable radio, matches, candles and flashlights. We stocked bottled
water, canned food, a manual can opener, crackers, and an assortment of
unperishable food items, guaranteed to last into the 22nd century, "just in
case".

Johnny and I were among the many people who were blissfully unaware of the steps being taken behind the scenes to ensure that this new technologically-generated world would enter the 21st century unscathed. In fact, as most of us were waiting for the midnight hour to arrive in our time zone, the folks involved in seeing that all went well in banking, utilities, hospitals, etc., had already been looking at New Zealand, the first to enter the new millennium.

When New Zealand survived Y2K, followed by Australia and the subsequent countries, the watchers in the United States began to stop holding their collective breath.

For us, New Year's Eve had often included watching the festivities in New York on television but this year would be different. We had no television. We also had no chairs or any of those things we had collected to prepare for a Y2K disaster "just in case". They were all sitting in boxes in French Lick at Michael T's Motel, and we were sitting on the floor of our apartment in Waterville, Ohio, listening to our little portable radio, waiting for the ball to drop at Times Square in New York.

Five.., four.., three.., two.., one.., "Happy New Year!" We were singing "Auld Lang Syne", silently clanking our Styrofoam cups, toasting in the New Year and the New Millennium with the wine that had been given to us by friends. Then we realized that our lights were still on; electricity still worked. The telephone rang, our kids wishing us "Happy New Year"; we could still communicate with the outside world. It looked like nothing had happened that had been anticipated by the modern world, however, something was about to happen in our lives, something that was beyond anything we had imagined.

The Little Red Chevette

The dawning of the 21st century was sunny and mild with the temperature hovering near 50 degrees. A perfect day for traveling but first we still had to pack the rest of our things that had not been sent ahead.

Our little red Chevette was a three-door subcompact with a hatchback that allowed us to carry some pretty big loads like lumber and piano actions, but our poor little car hadn't seen anything yet.

Johnny was blessed with the brain of an engineer. With this wonderful gift he could always envision intricate projects and designs and make the impossible happen....most of the time....but not that day. Even I could see that the amount of stuff that still needed to go to French Lick was far beyond what our little red Chevette could handle so I secretly telephoned Jeff while his father was at the gas station and cried, "HELP!" He arrived with a pickup truck and he and his father began stuffing stuff into the back of the little car. When it looked like the car was almost full they decided it was time for me to get into the passenger seat. As soon as I was buckled in, they started placing, packing, and pushing stuff around me.

I had stuff packed under and over my legs. My lap was holding *something*, I don't know what. My arms were so immobilized that I couldn't have scratched my nose. I felt like a china statue being taken to French Lick; all that was missing was bubble wrap and a big red stamp on my forehead that said, "FRAGILE".

After Jeff had loaded the 'excess baggage' that was still sitting on the sidewalk into his pickup, the car's passenger side door was slammed shut. I was there, and there I would stay, completely packed in with no chance of escaping. Not that I wanted to. They could have strapped me to the top of the car and I don't think I would have minded. After 41 years I was finally going BACK TO FRENCH LICK.

Our 40ᵗʰ Wedding Anniversary

This move from Ohio to Indiana had its beginning on October 3, 1998, when our family gave us the gift of celebrating our wedding anniversary at the French Lick Springs Hotel. They knew that of all the places in the world that Mom and Dad would like to go, it was to the place where two very young people met, fell in love and joined their lives 40 years before.

After our anniversary dinner and while the younger members of our family enjoyed the indoor activities of the hotel, the adults shared a bottle of Champaign in our room. Knowing that we had often spoken of moving back to French Lick "someday'" our children brought up this dream of ours and asked, "When are you planning to move?" We answered, "Someday." That was the answer they expected but not the answer they were willing to accept. They responded with, "Why not do it now while you are still young enough to enjoy it". Imagine how being called 'young' by our children at our 40th wedding anniversary made us feel. We started to see ourselves not old but almost fledgling-like, ready to hop out of the nest we had been in for so many years and try our wings in a new adventure. So, with this encouragement from our children and seeing that we had their blessings, we returned to our home in Ohio and began to take steps, albeit baby steps, toward moving into a new life in French Lick. Unbeknown to us, God was way ahead of us.

Less than a year later, in September of 1999, our dear friend, Bill Wright, invited us to join him in a concert at the First Baptist Church in West Baden Springs. We happily accepted. Bill was the "headliner"; Johnny played the accordion, the piano, and he and I sang. Jake Nicholson played the guitar and my high school classmates, Wayne and Ann Ferguson were also in the concert. Wayne sang, played the harmonica and was the master of ceremony. Ann planned the program and had the challenging job of keeping us on task. Johnny and I were so thrilled to be on the same program with such wonderful musicians.

I will forever remember my "little" brother, Tommie, who came with his family all the way from Tennessee to attend our concert, and my half-sister, Violet, with her hand raised in praise as we sang "When We All Get to Heaven". Vi has now joined the saints in heaven, departing this life at the age of 96.

At our rehearsal the day before the concert we mentioned to Ann and Wayne that we were *thinking* about returning to French Lick to live, *maybe* in the next year. Wayne hadn't heard the word 'maybe' so he announced to the audience at the concert that we *were* moving back to French Lick, *next year*.

Johnny took this as a 'sign' that we should quit talking and start doing, so he said to me, "Why don't we move the first of the year?" Sounded good to me.

Johnny and I were both in our early 60's and not wanting to retire. Johnny had his own business as a piano tuner and technician but he was hoping to concentrate only on playing the piano. When a gentleman who was well known in the piano music field heard Johnny play "How Great Thou Art" on the piano, he was very impressed and said to let him know when we came to town so he could put us in touch with someone who might want to hire Johnny as the pianist at their elegant restaurant.

At that time I was employed at a nursing center in Waterville, Ohio, as the Receptionist. In a surprising turn of events, our nursing center had recently been bought by the same company that owned the nursing center in French Lick.

Somewhere in the back of my mind I started to think that maybe, just maybe, this could somehow lead to our returning to French Lick. That hope had always been in my heart, hidden but not forgotten. I had heard of people 'visualizing' an outcome that they wanted to happen but I had never subscribed to that idea. However I came across an old postcard of the French Lick Springs Hotel that seemed to reach my very soul. Just looking at the picture of the hotel gave me a certain peace that I wanted to keep experiencing. I took the postcard to work with me and put it on my desk and every time I looked at the postcard I just had a good feeling.

While we were in town that September, I paid a visit to the administrator of the French Lick nursing facility. Lo and behold, he told me there would be an opening in the office around the first of the year and I could just transfer, not losing any seniority. This was really working out beautifully. So with everything falling into place we headed back home to Waterville to start wrapping up our lives there and planning for the future move.

There were varied responses from friends and family about this 'change of life' we were going through, everything from, "Are you wanting to starve to death?", from my Uncle Duke to, "You guys are my heroes.", from our son Jeff. The most important people, our children, were supportive and that was all that mattered, so we stepped out on faith and proceeded with our plans.

Sometimes I think God tricked us into going to French Lick. He led us to believe that He was fulfilling OUR plans when all along He had much better plans waiting for us.

The first indication that things were not going along as *we* had planned came when my 'for-sure' job wasn't sure anymore. The person I was to replace decided not to leave after all. I thought this might be the end of our moving but Johnny said, "We ARE going." He didn't get any argument from me. So our step of faith turned out to be a giant leap.

Chapter 2

"I'll Take You Home Again, Kathleen"

When we arrived in French Lick on this first night of the New Year and saw the lights of the hotel shining through the light fog on this unusually warm midnight, we had the eerie feeling that we had just stepped back to 1958. Johnny started singing "I'll Take You Home Again Kathleen" just like he did back in the early morning hours when we would be driving to my parents' house to visit on his day off from playing in Louisville, KY, with the Ted Huston Orchestra or later when we returned from Buffalo, NY, where the Orchestra had spent the winter playing at the Statler-Hilton Hotel. Johnny had resigned from the orchestra at the end of the Buffalo engagement because we were expecting our first baby that summer and had decided to settle down to a more normal life. He didn't sing the whole song, he didn't need to. We both knew the line, "To where your heart has ever been, since, first you were my bonnie bride". I use to think he was singing that for me, knowing how much I wanted to come 'home', but looking back, I think he was singing it as much for himself as for me. He loved French Lick and I believe he was never as happy and at ease as he was while working in the French Lick and West Baden Springs Hotels. Even though he was born in Michigan and grew up in Ohio I think it is safe to say that Johnny was a "born-again Hoosier". As for me, I never will consider myself anything but a Hoosier, no matter what my address may be.

Sunday, our first full day in French Lick, we decided to run up to Paoli, nine miles away, to do a little shopping at Wal-Mart. We were in the back of the store when I heard someone yell, "Gramma!" Every grandmother in the store instinctively looked around including me and to my astonishment and utter delight, there was my granddaughter, Jodie, who should have been in northwestern Ohio, coming towards me and giving me a big hug. Our son John had brought her and some of the things that hadn't made it into our little Chevette. Eagle-eyed Jodie had spotted our little red Chevette in the Wal-Mart's parking lot as they were driving past the store in route to French Lick. Now I didn't feel so far away from our family.

~

Georgia Dixon had been one of my best friends in high school. Her family had moved into the house right across the street from our house sometime during our high school years. Georgia had lived at our home during part of our senior year when both of us were dating boys who went to the same college. We would sit on our twin beds at night, dressed in our pajamas, and write exact letters to them…we thought we were sooooo clever. Georgia later married my second cousin, Jack Dixon, so now we were not only friends but relatives. Even though we went our different ways, she to Indianapolis, Indiana, and I to Waterville, Ohio, whenever we would get together it was as if we had never been apart.

Jack and Georgia invited us to their home for dinner that first Sunday night. Georgia worked at the hotel's spa and thought there might be a retail job for me at the hotel in the Panache dress shop. She told me to go fill out an application the next day. I wasn't thrilled with the idea of working in a dress shop, retail isn't something I enjoy, but I needed a job.

~

On Monday, January 3rd Johnny and I awoke to another warm but rainy day. If this was the weather we were going to have down here in southern Indiana that was okay with us. So the first thing I did was follow Georgia's advice and go to the hotel to apply for a job.

There was a small guard house at the start of the road leading to the employees' entrance and I told the security guard that I was there to apply for a job. He allowed me to go on down the road to the Hotel's employees' entrance. This road ran behind the power plant and as I walked down the road I couldn't take my eyes off the power plant door where my father, Frank McDonald, had walked through every day, and I mean *every* day, with very few exceptions, to begin his workday as the Chief Engineer.

When I got to the employees' entrance I stopped at the office and said, "I would like to apply for a job."

The security guard picked up the phone and I heard him say, "Eva Sharron McDonald is here to fill out an application."

Wait a minute, I didn't remember telling him my name, but he knew me, AND he used my maiden name. I squinted to read his name tag and saw a familiar name, Rex Drabing, who I remembered as "Dutch" Drabing. Even though he had been a few years ahead of me in school I remembered that he had played basketball when he was in high school. In French Lick, basketball players were the "rock stars" of the school, the town, and everyone knew their names. Now "Dutch" remembered me, what a surprise.

The Human Resource person who brought an application to me was Cindy, a niece to my friend Georgia's husband, Jack. In fact, my grandmother and her great-grandmother had been sisters.

And by the way, knowing who your grandparents or great-grand parents were is important in French Lick. As in many small towns, lineage matters. You start to realize that you are not just *you* but a continuation of parents, grandparents, great-grandparents, ad infinitum. I think this exhibits a look into a small town's values, something much deeper than idle curiosity. I see it as respect for family.

~

When I finished filling out the application, Cindy began my interview. I don't remember any of the questions or even if she asked me any, but somewhere in the middle of the interview I began to realize that she was talking about their concierge leaving at the end of the week and I could have that job. She seemed to already know about my father's many years of employment at the hotel and that I had grown up in French Lick, so she said, "You know all about the hotel and its history, and you can answer all the history questions that guests ask".

It slowly began to soak in that I had just been hired….I had a job. Cindy said I would start on Wednesday to be trained by the current concierge. Just image, I came to French Lick on January 1st with no job and no prospect of a job and here I was, starting a new job on January 5th. How is that for timing?

After announcing my good news to Johnny that I would begin my new job in two days, we decided that now would be a good time to go to Jasper and pick up a few things we needed.

Jasper is a small city located about 25 miles southwest of French Lick. While in Jasper the weather became stormy so we cut short our shopping trip and headed back to French Lick. We later learned that we had been feeling the effects of two F-3 tornados that had ripped through northeastern Kentucky, hitting Owensboro, Kentucky, the hardest with winds sometimes reaching 100 MPH that afternoon. Owensboro is less than 44 miles from Jasper.

After dropping off what we had bought in Jasper and being oblivious to the severe weather we went to Paoli to finish our shopping. Little did we know how much we were tempting fate.

When we returned to the valley from Paoli the road through West Baden was closed due to flooding. We HAD to get to French Lick so we made the decision to go through the high water…slowly and carefully. Johnny drove and I prayed. By the grace of God we made it. Now we were starting to remember what southern Indiana weather *really* could be like.

First Day of Training

When I had last seen the hotel it was the French Lick Sheraton Hotel. The floor of the lobby had been covered with large black and white linoleum-type squares, a band stand had been at the north end of the lobby, and hanging from the ceiling in the lobby had been birdcage-style lights. The furnishings had included low back armless chairs and black and white tables that blended in with the black and white floor, shin high as I painfully remember. But what met my eyes that day was a lobby that reflected an earlier time, long before the hotel that I had last seen. This was my first glimpse of the past that I would be seeing more clearly in the coming years. I had no idea that the beginning of the 21st century would reveal the beginning of the 20th century.

And They Knew Me When

The young lady who trained me showed me around to all the shops and dining rooms in the building plus the Presidential Suite and Governor's Suite that had once been the homes of Tom Taggart, the builder of the hotel in 1901, and his son Thomas D. Taggart, respectively. Then she took me to the Pro Shop and introduced me to several employees there. One gentleman, James Carter, surprised me when he said, "I use to work for your dad." He went on to tell the other men in the pro shop, "At one time over half the men in Orange County worked for her dad." Then he continued, "One time we had a water leak but no one knew where the pipes were. Frank McDonald just walked out in the middle of the front lawn, pointed to a spot on the lawn, and said, "Dig here", and he was right. You would have had to be a squirrel to know right where that pipe was."

As the day went by I began meeting people that I remembered from my school days. I also met other long-time employees who not only had known my father, but remembered my mother; my half brother, Harold; my brother, Tommie; half-sisters, Opal, Violet and June; and various aunts, uncles, cousins and friends. I had spent the past forty years living where no one "knew me when" and now it seemed as if *everyone* "knew me when".

AND they called me Eva Sharron

My name has been a problem for me beginning when I left the security of my hometown and entered Indiana University. Most people, if asked their name can say, "Mary" or "Ann", or even "Mary Ann", and that will be the end of it. For me, my name always seems to require some sort of explanation.

To begin with, "Eva" usually requires explaining that the 'E' is short, *eh*, as in *E*vansville. I was named for Tom Taggart, Jr.'s daughter, Eva, who was named for her grandmother, Eva Bryant Taggart. Both women pronounced their names with a short *e*.

With "Sharron" I have to give a spelling lesson. I don't have to worry about the number of 'r's unless it is being written on something important. Then I need to advise that there are two r's in Sharron. Those two 'r's are the fault of the sisters at St. Edward's Hospital in New Albany, Indiana, where I was born. They told my mother that *Sharon* is a place or a flower and *Sharron* is person's name. My mother took them at their word, even though she was not a Catholic and would never take anything else a Catholic said as 'gospel'.

My maiden surname is "McDonald", written with a short line under the "c" to represent the missing "a", just in case the "a" *is* missing, because according to my father, the clan McDonald, or clan MacDonald, one being Scottish and one being Irish, I'm never sure which, moved around a lot between Ireland and Scotland (probably trying to avoid being massacred), thus making us Scots-Irish or Scotch-Irish, and I'm not sure which of those is proper either, whew.

As if that wasn't enough, my married surname is "Kobee", not "Kobe" or "Colby". When my father-in-law was only 12 years old he came all alone to the United States from his home country, Austria. His surname was spelled "Kobe", but because people were not pronouncing the 'e' he just added the second 'e' to hear the correct pronunciation.

And, there is more, I grew up being called by both names, Eva Sharron. Daddy was the exception, he only called me Eva. There isn't a hyphen on my birth certificate but according to Mother there should have been. And now you can understand why I sometimes wish my name had been just plain "Jane"'. I'm serious.

One time I happened to mention to my mother that I would have liked to have been named Jane and she said, "I wanted to name you Sharron Jane but Daddy wanted you to be named Eva". Maybe I had heard that in utero.

I had a psychiatrist tell me that I needed to decide who I was and insist on being called by that name. I tried following his advice, first using only "Eva" but I STILL had to explain the pronunciation. Then I tried being just "Sharron". That worked pretty well until we moved back to French Lick.

The folks who 'knew me when' called me by both names and I began to feel as if I had *finally* regained my identity, having now come full circle.

(Please note that I have used almost two pages explaining about my name.......I'll bet you also wish Mother had named me *Jane.)*

chapter 3

How Do You Spell "Concierge?"

By Friday, the third day of my employment I was turned loose, on my own as *concierge*.

The first thing I did was introduced myself to the secretary for the General Manager and ask her if she had a dictionary I could borrow. She graciously offered me one and we chatted for a short time. As I was leaving, I casually asked her, "How do you spell `concierge'?" She spelled it out for me: c-o-n-c-i-e-r-g-e. I thanked her and walked back to the lobby and to my desk.

In the Bible, Proverbs 17:28, Solomon says "Even fools are thought wise if they keep silent". Well, for once I had kept silent and I guess I appeared to know what I was being hired to do….but I had no idea what a *concierge* was or how to be one.

As soon as I sat down at my desk I looked up *concierge* in the dictionary and the first descriptive word was *"Slave"*. I have often joked when I've told this story saying that I figured I had the right qualifications after having been married over 40 years. Following the word "slave" was *"a hotel employee whose job is to assist guests by arranging tours, making reservations, etcetera"*. There it was, my job description. That didn't give me much to go on but it was a start. Some weeks later I found the movie *For Love or Money* at the public library. I borrowed it and as Johnny and I watched the movie I looked at him and asked in wonderment, "Is *THAT* what I am?" He just shrugged; he didn't know what a *concierge* was either.

That movie was my only look at a concierge, my training film so to speak. The character, Doug Ireland, who was played by Michael J. Fox, really inspired me and I concluded that if a guest had a problem that must mean that I had a problem and if a guest needed something I needed to see that they got it.

Shortly after viewing the movie a guest called my desk to say that he needed a tooth brush. I brightly said, "I'll get one for you right away." I thought about running to the drug store and buying one and then thought again…..maybe the hotel has them. So I called 'someone', I don't remember who, and they told me to call 'someone' else, and they told me to call yet another 'someone' else. The third call was to housekeeping and housekeeping took a toothbrush to the guest. Now I had learned two valuable lessons: who to call to get a toothbrush, and that it would ALWAYS take three calls to reach the right person.

I suffered through many embarrassing moments but I learned. One of those moments came during my first month on the job. I had been told that afternoon tea, which was offered only on Saturday, was discontinued during the month of January.

Guests would come to my desk asking about the tea and I would give them the information that we would not be serving in January. One Saturday afternoon a guest came to me and asked, "What time will tea be served?" I answered, "I'm sorry but we are not serving tea today." She then sarcastically asked, "Is *that* the tea that is *not* being served today?" as she pointed to something behind me. I turned around and saw that a server was setting up the table for tea and cookies. No one had bothered to inform me of the change of plans. Now I learned that it was *my* responsibility to know what was and what was not going on.

My love for the hotel quickly made me want every guest to have a wonderful time at our hotel and I wanted to do all that I could to make that happen.

I had never had any training in hospitality per se, but I remembered when I was in grade school seeing written above the blackboard, "The Golden Rule" from Matthew 7:12 – reminding me that I should treat other people the way I want to be treated. That is what hospitality really is and you can't help seeing that scripture day after day, year after year, without it making some kind of an impact.

Before guests started to arrive that first week-end I had some quiet time to sit and think. I was just looking all around the lobby when I glanced up to the ceiling and my eyes settled on the crystal chandeliers. I seemed to remember them being in the dining room back in 1958, and my father telling me they were made in Germany, prior to World War II. He said replacement parts could not be obtained anymore because, "We bombed the factory."

As I continued to absorb my surroundings I suddenly realized that my desk was in the exact place where my desk had been when I was the Social Hostess, 42 years before. For all I knew, this could be the same desk; its vintage seemed to be from the Sheraton years. This really gave me a jolt, talk about Déjà vu.

Besides having a phone list of various departments, there was a rack of brochures of points of interest in the area… that was it. So I sat there trying to look like I knew something.

"Oh, God, why didn't you let me have that job at the nursing home?"

I was terrified.

While sitting at my desk, smiling, praying that no one would ask me anything, I started noticing a vaguely familiar odor wafting down the east hall but I just couldn't quite put my finger (or nose, as it were) on it. As I was puzzling over it a lady approached me and asked, "What is that smell?" All I could think of was that it might be coming from the salon where they could be giving perms. I gave that explanation and she seemed satisfied. Okay, I made it through the first question and started to feel like maybe I could actually pull this off. However, after a few more guests asked the same question I decided it was time for me to go a little further in this *concierge* thing, start stretching my wings so to speak, and be a problem solver. My thought was that those people in the salon could at least close their door so the other guests would not be offended by the odor. I took a deep breath, squared my shoulders and marched down to the end of the hall…. only to find that the salon was closed. That is when I had my *Aha* moment – that odor was Pluto water. They were giving Pluto water baths in the spa. I thought I would never forget that smell but apparently I was wrong. Once identified, I returned to my desk in the lobby, settled back, took a deep breath and just enjoyed the nostalgia the smell offered.

The odor of Pluto water is not offensive to me, it just brings back memories of a very happy time in an enchanted place where squirrels scampered, cat-birds called and my mother and I enjoyed many hot, lazy, summer afternoons.

The Sawdust Paths

I don't remember ever being inside the hotel when I was a child but sometimes on a summer afternoon while the hotel guests were eating lunch in the dining room, my mother and I would get dressed up in pretty, crisp summer dresses and walk down to the hotel's gardens. I remember walking through a big open archway built into the wall that separated the front of the hotel from the gardens. When we walked through that entrance it was as if we had stepped into another world. The paths in the Japanese garden were covered with sawdust and every so often I would need to stop walking, bend my knee and tap my toe on the ground behind me to get the sawdust out of my sandal. Mother would bring peanuts that were in their shells so I could feed the squirrels and chipmunks. I would laugh at the little chipmunks when they stuffed their mouths with so many nuts that it looked like their little cheeks might burst. But I didn't like it when the blue jays dive-bombed for one of the nuts I had tossed to a little squirrel. The cat birds were a favorite of mine, with their soft gray feathers and the way they sounded like a cat meowing. We would watch the gold fish swimming in the pond and darting under the water lily pads. I felt as if I were in a very special place as I walked across the little white bridges that spanned the child sized lakes. This whole area was quiet and peaceful. The smell of the Pluto water only added to the sense of otherworldliness.

Yes, I actually *liked* the smell of Pluto water then and I still do. Of course Pluto water has an odor; it is teeming with minerals that God has given this good earth, minerals that are necessary for our bodies. Personally, when I have smelled Pluto or any mineral water I associate it with being outdoors, nature, and enjoyment. Don't get me wrong, I love the smell of lavender, lilacs, carnations, roses, cinnamon, sweet basil, mint and lots of pleasant scents but I also like to smell the things that identify my surroundings: new mown grass and hay, a horse barn, the fishy smell of the river, and the warm smells of a high school gym at a basketball game. I want to not only *see* and *hear* my surroundings, I want to *smell* my surroundings, too.

Behind the hotel were the formal gardens and in the summer they were always in full bloom. There was a sun dial in the middle of the garden that was inscribed with a saying that Mr. Tom Taggart, Sr. had authored. It read, "Time and Pluto Wait for No Man". I thought it was so clever to know the time by that sundial and had to check it out during every visit to the gardens.

As we started our walk home pass the Power Plant, Daddy would sometimes meet us for a brief visit. These summer afternoons would end with a stop at the Rexall Drug Store that was across the street from the Plant. Mother and I would each have a dish of vanilla ice cream with pineapple topping.

Questions and Lots of Them

It didn't take long before I was hearing a variety of questions from guests: "How old is this hotel?" "Was *The Shining* filmed here"? "Why is this town called French Lick?", and one of my all-time favorites, "Are those chandeliers from the *Titanic?*"

When a question came up that I as yet didn't know the answer, I turned to other members of the staff, particularly the bellmen, who had been answering these same types of questions for years. With what I was learning from the staff and the bits and pieces I was beginning to remember from my own past I was getting by.

But I didn't want to just "get by", I wanted to really know about the history and, as I was discovering, so did our guests.

Necessity Becomes a Passion

Learning about the hotel's history began as a necessity, after all hadn't I been hired because, "*You know all about the hotel and its history, and you can answer all the history questions that guests ask.*"? But the hotel's history quickly became my passion.

During my brief two-day training the concierge had shown me a room on the lower floor of the hotel, that I equated with a dungeon, where decorations for parties were stored. There were also some file cabinets in that room that had papers about the hotel's past activities. Weekdays were rather slow so I started bringing some of the papers, a few at a time, up to my desk in the lobby so I could study them during my downtime. I wasn't sure what I was searching for but I couldn't just sit and do nothing. These papers started giving me a look back at the hotel and the more I read the more I became captivated by the hotel's past.

I discovered several historical accounts relating to the hotel's history and often I found varying information as to what was fact and what was folk lore. I really wanted to pass on true information, not fables. Just any old answer would not do.

I would walk through the halls taking care to notice how one area looked differently from another, giving me clues about the hotel's history.

I looked at the exterior of the hotel to see the placement of bricks and the adding of stained glass, noting when wings and floors were added.

I began thinking how my father would have seen this hotel grow and wishing I could have been in his shoes. Little did I imagine that this wish would one day be granted.

Chapter 4

Home Hunting

When we were preparing to move to French Lick we chose to find a temporary home until we decided where we wanted to settle down. Our hope was to become permanent residents. As Johnny would say, "We're here for the duration."

One day we were shopping at a small market just outside of West Baden and as we were paying for our groceries the clerk asked us to sign our receipt and drop it in a box that was sitting on the counter. I don't remember which one of us asked what the box was for but the clerk said it was a drawing for a trip to Hawaii. Without missing a beat Johnny said, "No thanks, we like it here." We didn't participate. (God forbid we would have to leave French Lick and go visit Hawaii) Our kids still think that is one of the funniest things they ever heard of their dad saying.

We chose to start out at MICHAEL T'S MOTEL, located on the summit of one of the hills surrounding the French Lick Valley. They had a large room that would accommodate us and all of our "stuff. This proved to be an interesting experience. During bass fishing season the room was sometimes used by several bass fishermen on weekends. The size of the room accommodated four or more beds. For us the owners had supplied us with one bed, a small couch, a refrigerator and microwave. This room was not only our home; it was our storage unit as well.

Before we moved we gave our children most of our things that had any sentimental value, things they might want when we were gone, I mean really 'gone'. We did bring our dining room table and chairs, some additional tables, a dresser and a few other odds and ends. We didn't have a stove so we cooked in an electric fry pan. Johnny was the 'chef' in the family and he would surprise me with all kinds of tasty dishes; from goulash to meat loaf. We lined up our boxes to represent walls, separating our "bedroom" from our "living room" from our "kitchen".

We learned to adapt but one of the most difficult things was adapting to not being able to get away from each other. When we lived in Ohio we had our own business and we loved working together but that did not put us always in the same room. Now we were living in one giant room and this presented a problem we had never before encountered. When one of us felt the need to be alone we had to either go outside in the cold, or into the bathroom, the preferred place, because it was warm. However, if we were having a "discussion", the bathroom wasn't very helpful. The door to the bathroom was a sliding door that was only fastened at the top, and it is really hard to emphasize one's righteous anger by slamming a door when, no matter how hard you shoved it, that door just made a weak swishing sound as it closed, not the big, attention getting BANG that served as the last word plus explanation point!

Our West Baden Springs Home

In March a friend told us about a mobile home that was available in West Baden so we quickly called the owner. I mentioned my maiden name and she made the connection with members of my family she had known and offered for us to see the home. We took one look at the home and rented it.

We were able to move in rather quickly since we really didn't have much in the way of furniture.

The first day after we moved in, Johnny was standing at one end of our 'new' home and I was at the other end when Johnny yelled, "Hey, you look small." That was the farthest we had been apart for two months.

Indiana's State Symbols

Every time Johnny and I came to the 'Welcome to Indiana' sign, whether we were entering from Ohio or Kentucky, we would sing "Back Home Again, in Indiana". Upon reentry to Ohio we sang, "Beautiful Ohio". It is interesting to note that both of these songs had the same lyricist, Ballard MacDonald.

"Back Home Again, In Indiana" is not the official Indiana state song but is likely just as popular. Published in January of 1917, this song has been sung to open the Indianapolis 500 since 1946, with Jim Nabors singing it from 1972 till his final performance in 2014.

The official Indiana state song, "On the Banks of the Wabash, Far Away" was written by Paul Dresser in 1897. Mr. Dresser was from Terra Haute, Indiana and he must have seen a lot of sycamore trees along the banks of the Wabash River that is the border between Illinois and Indiana at Terra Haute. The Indiana General Assembly adopted "On the Banks of the Wabash, Far Away" as the state song on March 14, 1913 and it was the first official symbol of Indiana, four years before the state flag was adopted. According to Historic Landmark's Foundation of Indiana, Mr. Dresser is said to have composed this song while staying at the West Baden Springs Hotel and was first performed by waiter, George Higby. This must have been at the original wood frame hotel before it was destroyed in the fire of 1901. In both songs, "The Banks of the Wabash" and "Back Home Again, in Indiana" we find the words; 'Wabash' 'moonlight', 'gleaming', 'candle lights', 'fields', 'new-mown hay', and, of course, 'sycamores', and that pretty much says it all.

If I were to write a song about a tree in Indiana I think I would write about the cedar tree. The first cedar I ever saw was our Christmas tree. The cedar is that wonderful evergreen that seems to be able to survive anywhere. As you drive along the highways in southern Indiana that have been cut through limestone you can sometimes see these trees standing on what appears to be solid rock. As a Hoosier who has lived the majority her life (so far) in Ohio, I have sometimes thought about the cedar tree that can take root and grow in only a tiny bit of soil and been encouraged to grow where God has planted me even when I didn't feel like I had much to stand on.

The first sycamore trees that I really noticed were not in Indiana, but in Farnsworth Park near our home in Waterville, Ohio, where my husband, Johnny, and I use to enjoy walking. It is a very narrow park that is bordered on one side by the Anthony Wayne Trail and on the other side by the Maumee River. The Anthony Wayne Trail had once been part of the Miami and Erie Canals system that carried boats loaded with produce, livestock and people, including soldiers being transported from Toledo to Cincinnati for the Mexican War in 1845. The canal was filled in sometime around the 1930's and became Old U.S. 24/The Anthony Wayne Trail.

The footpath in the park goes all the way to the town of Grand Rapids, Ohio, about ten miles from Waterville. It was on my bucket list to walk the entire length from Waterville to Grand Rapids but we never got farther than three miles into the park. That was really enough because those walks were so pleasurable and emotionally soothing that Johnny would sometimes say to me when one of us was having a particularly hard day, "We need to go for a walk.", and as we had walked, life began to take on a whole new appearance.

On evening as we were walking, an animal stepped out from behind a clump of trees and crossed our path. At first we thought it looked like a very unkempt dog. Then we realized we had just seen our first coyote. That place in the path was thereafter referred to as 'Coyote Crossing' by us.

In the front yard of our home in West Baden there stood a big sycamore tree. The sycamore tree is mentioned in Indiana's state song, however, the tulip tree, or yellow poplar, is the state's official tree.

There was a tulip tree just across the road from the sycamore tree. I remember seeing my first tulip tree when I was little and I was playing in a yard out in the country where my family was attending a funeral. The children were sent outside to play and not bother the grown-ups. It was very hot and we were playing in the shade of a big tree. There was a nice breeze rustling the leaves of the tree and I happened to look up and was surprised to see what looked like tulips growing at the top of the tree. When I told my parents about the tree they said, "That is Indiana's state tree." I was so proud to be part of a state that had such a wonderful tree as its very own.

We had moved to West Baden in early spring when the trees were just beginning to produce their leaves. One morning as I was standing at my kitchen window I noticed a tree whose leaves looked somehow familiar. As I studied the tree it finally dawned on me that this was a buckeye tree. So, we had Indiana in the front of our home and Ohio in the back. Rather symbolic, don't you think?

That summer when our son John and daughter-in-law Holly brought their family to visit, their sons, Johnnie and Beau, collected buckeyes to take back to Ohio. (Sort of like taking coals to Newcastle).

Of all the places we had lived, our home in West Baden offered the most abundance of wild life. Every morning the squirrels would pull on their heavy combat boots, drop onto our tin roof with a big *thud* and clomp around above our bedroom until they were sure they had awoken us….at least that is what it sounded like to me.

After they got me awake, I would go to the kitchen, open the curtains, and there in the buckeye tree would be squirrels stationed on various limbs, staring at my kitchen window. When their little beady eyes saw me they scampered to our back porch where they knew I would be putting their "treats".

From the big bay window in our kitchen we could watch those little critters steal the corn that had been put out for the birds.

We became kitchen-table bird watchers as we enjoyed seeing a plethora of cardinals, robins, blue Jays and rusty blackbirds in our yard. One day we were so excited to identify a pileated woodpecker. It didn't take much to excite us. At night I loved hearing a whip-poor-will or a screech-owl serenade us. I even saw my very first, honest-to-goodness blue bird one day when I was walking in West Baden.

The deer were quite prevalent in West Baden. Not only did they take ownership of the West Baden Hotel grounds, they felt that all of West Baden was their home. While sitting on our porch in the evening, we would see deer come strolling past our house on the sidewalk right in front of us, without a care in the world.

When the lowland across from our home would flood, a groundhog seeking higher ground sometimes came to stay temporarily under our shed. Every day I would see the groundhog sitting on his haunches, surveying the flood situation, watching for dry land so he could return to his home across the street. Not seeing any, he would crawl back under the shed and wait for the next day to repeat his lookout for dry land. Once land appeared we wouldn't see him again until the next flood.

There was a little canal across the street where blue heron would fish and ducks liked to swim. One day a dog saw a duck family; Momma, Daddy, and babies, swimming along and decided to go after them. Daddy Duck took over as protector of the family and kept the dog busy chasing him so Momma and babies could get away. The dog finally got tired and gave up the chase. Good for you, Daddy Duck.

I enjoy seeing all of God's creatures, well, almost all, but not snakes. I have no problem with lizards or spiders, maybe a little skittish when it comes to anything with feathers. I love to look at birds but I cannot touch them. However, show me a snake and I freak out. I can't even look at a picture of a snake without cringing, squeezing my eyes shut, turning my head and feeling nauseous. One of the nice things about living in northwestern Ohio was that in the forty years that I lived there I never saw a snake outside of the Toledo Zoo and I chose to not see them there.

Prior to moving to French Lick/West Baden we had been apartment dwellers for several years so that first May when we now had a place where I could do some gardening I decided to plant flowers in our front yard. But as I was getting started I discovered a dead snake, or part of a dead snake, lying in my yard. It looked like it had been run over by the lawn mower. I ran to the end of our block to the street department men and reported the dead snake. They sat there looking at me, not seeming to grasp the urgency of my situation, so I had to tell them again, "There is a dead snake in my front yard." They still didn't seem to get it, so I said again, enunciating each word, "I-can't-go-in-my-yard-be-cause-there-is-a-**dead**-**snake**-in-it." Now they understood. A nice man who worked for the street department moseyed up the sidewalk to my front yard while I stayed a very safe distance from my home. He picked up what was left of the culprit's corpse with a stick, and flung it into the field that was across from our home. It was now safe for me to go in my yard and plant flowers.

The following spring we were working in our yard, getting rid of leaves and debris that had accumulated during the winter. I was raking leaves away from the back of the house when I saw what looked like a rolled-up piece of black tire that had reddish-orange on the inside. I took a really close look to see what it was and screamed, "Johnny! SNAKE"!, and I ran inside. Since this was early March and still cold, that poor snake must have been rolled up trying to keep warm under the pile of leaves. It didn't even unroll when I disturbed its dormancy. Johnny called me as he was bringing it around the house, "Honey, come and look at this snake. What kind is it?"

"It's a **SNAKE.**" I had looked at it long enough to know THAT and I didn't need to know more. He took it across the street to where the partial snake had been tossed the summer before. Sometime later I read in a little book by A. J. Rhodes about the early history of our valley where he tells about black snakes with red bellies found in the swamp around the mineral waters in the French Lick area. I think that may have been what I saw that day.

The area across from our home was where several mineral springs had once been but were no longer flowing. However, when it rained we often had 'lake-front' property. I could see things that looked like sticks floating in the water. When I ask a man from the street department what they were he gave me a look, and said, "You don't want to know".

About a year later there was a live black snake in our yard. Fortunately I was not at home at the time and Johnny was the one who discovered it. Somehow the street department guys got involved, again. After surrounding the creature it was decided that for my sake they would relocate this snake to what was becoming a snake depository across the street. His life was spared. Interestingly, not long after, we had a mouse move into our home. Apparently Mr. Black Snake was living beneath our home, (ugh), feeding on mice. Well, give me a mouse any day over a snake.

And while we are on the slithery subject of snakes, when our daughter, Julie, was five and had just returned from her kindergarten field trip to the Toledo Zoo, she, being the oldest and wisest of her siblings saw her opportunity for a "teaching moment" (she gets that from me). She was enthusiastically telling her four year old brother, John Michael, about all the animals she had just seen at the zoo. She told of the lions and tigers and bears, "Oh my!" (Sorry, I just couldn't resist). John Michael was playing it cool; his only response was a shake of his little towhead while uttering a negative grunt, no matter what she tried to tell him, and this only made her more determined to impress him. When she got to the snakes at the zoo she kept emphasizing that the snakes were REALLY BIG. John refused to believe her, persisting in his negative grunt until she sealed the matter with, "John, those snakes were so big they had to roll 'em up to get 'em in the cage!" There.

Chapter 5

Two Hotels – Two Tours

Johnny and I soon discovered that the love for history seemed to permeate the valley. Wherever people gathered, invariably the subject of the history of either French Lick or West Baden Springs would come up. I figured that there were more historians per square foot in Orange County than anywhere else in Indiana. The fact that the West Baden Hotel had received a new breath of life puffed back into it through the efforts of Bill and Gayle Cook and Historic Landmarks Foundation of Indiana, was not only reviving the West Baden Spring Hotel, but was starting to slowly resuscitate the entire valley.

The West Baden Hotel Tour

Not long after we moved to West Baden, Johnny was offered the opportunity to be a tour guide at the West Baden Springs Hotel for Historic Landmarks of Indiana. This was before the hotel had been fully restored. He loved learning the history of the building and all of the facts about saving the structure. He found the stories about Lee Sinclair and Ed Ballard fascinating and developed a real passion for giving tours, sharing the information that Historic Landmarks had researched. But he especially respected and appreciated what Bill and Gail Cook were doing for the West Baden Springs Hotel. Johnny and I were blessed to have spent time talking with them on several occasions, getting to know these warm, caring people.

⁓

The French Lick Hotel Tour

When the previous concierge was showing me around, the notion that the tour needed to be far more than just pointing out venues started to form in my mind. I began to envision a tour that included the history of the hotel; after all, everything about the hotel seemed to speak to me of its glorious past.

While creating a history tour of the French Lick Springs Hotel had been my idea, I wasn't sure what one looked like. At that point in time I had never been on a history tour, not even the Historic Landmarks Tour at the West Baden Hotel.

When I approached our General Manager, Dominique Audran, with my idea, vague as it was, of promoting our hotel's rich history by giving a "Hotel History Tour", he was very receptive to the concept and told me to just tell him what I needed. I had seen pictures of the hotel's past in the rooms below the lobby and I got the idea to use those pictures in the tour. They were placed haphazardly with no rhyme or reason so I asked M. Audran if I could have them rearranged in chronological order. He gave his permission and the first step was taken for the tour.

I began by offering the history tour to anyone who showed an interest in our history; all they had to do was ask one little question about the hotel's past and I would eagerly offer them a History Tour. An unsuspecting guest sitting quietly in the lobby also became easy prey as I swooped down to snatch someone to take on a tour.

The Buffalo Rock

Most of the time guests were happy to join me, so I was surprised when a guest whom I was trying to coerce into going on one of my tours told me he didn't need to go because he had already been in the garden and seen the rock that the buffalo had licked.

I didn't know there was such a rock on the French Lick hotel grounds but then again I was still new to this job. I didn't want to let on that I had no idea what he was talking about so I just said something like, "Oh, okay.", and I backed off.

My imagination took me to expect a large rock comparable to the "Roche de Boeuf" at Waterville, Ohio, where we had lived before coming back to French Lick.

That "Roche de Boeuf" is a large outcropping of limestone that was so named by French fur traders who, as the story goes, thought it looked like a large chunk of beef, or a buffalo, naming it "Buffalo Rock".

Folklore tells us that on this rock, Native Americans held councils before the Battle of Fallen Timbers in 1794 and that Anthony Wayne had camped at Fort Deposit on a high bank opposite the Roche de Boeuf for two days before that battle. With all of this in mind, I quickly went out to the garden to search for French Lick's "Roche de Boeuf". And there, a few feet from the Pluto Spring I found "The Rock". It was a stone monument, a rock, that the Daughters of the American Revolution had placed in the garden to memorialize the blockhouse or fort that had been in use between 1812 and 1815 and was on the property now owned by the French Lick Springs Hotel. There are indentations all over the rock and this gentleman had misunderstood the whole message on the plaque that is attached to the rock, thinking that the indentations were caused by those big beasts licking salt off of that rock.

Yes, that was an amusing story but it was not an isolated muddling of information. No, I never had anyone else come up with that particular idea but some were just as absurd and often came by way of people who, like me, were just repeating what was common lore.

As I continued developing the French Lick Hotel History Tour I tried to find out the truth and tell it, keeping integrity as my focus. I also tried to avoid telling about the history of the West Baden Hotel; they had their own tour that was scripted by Historic Landmarks of Indiana. When guests asked about the West Baden Hotel I encouraged them to take that tour.

We had so much fun with our respective tours. I would tell my guests to be sure to go on the West Baden tour and to say, "Hello" to Johnny, and Johnny would tell his guests to come over to the French Lick Hotel and go on my tour. Guests seemed to like the way we were promoting each other's hotel tours and would often comment that they had just been on the other hotel's tour. Johnny and I knew that guests were here to enjoy our hotels; they didn't want to hear anything that would cast disparagement on the "other" hotel.

After that winter of finding my footing, the tour began to almost take on a life all its own and by summer we had a Hotel History Tour. Of course availability of points of interest, size of the group, and weather conditions had to be taken into account, but basically each tour covered the same ground, just sometimes in a different order.

~

Since I started the tour from the lobby, that was our first point of interest. I would tell about the laying of the beautiful mosaic tile floor by Italian artisans in 1901, and how Sheraton had covered the floor with large black and white tiles in the 1950's.

The Sheraton Corporation endeavored to bring the hotel up to what was the style of the "fabulous fifties". Shortly after purchasing the hotel, Sheraton closed for three months to remodel. Ceilings were lowered, chandeliers were replaced with "modern" light fixtures, brass fixtures were painted over, and the connection between Pluto and the devil was promoted by naming two bars "Lucifer's Lounge" and "The Demon's Den". The hotel reopened in March, 1955, and business began to boom.

As we walked down the hall to the spa, the floor that was covered with carpet made a creaking sound and some guests would show concern that the floor was going to break. This gave me the opportunity to explain that what they were hearing were the black and white tiles from the Sheraton era, covering the mosaic tiles from the Taggart era, covering a wood floor. We got to *hear* history along with *seeing* history.

After a walk to the spa, and if available, to see some of the rooms in the spa, we would proceed to the lower lever to see the pictures of the past and learn more of the history behind the pictures.

I would use those pictures when giving a tour as a guide, reading the facts that were printed under the pictures and then expounding on that information. Before long I was recalling facts and personal anecdotes that had been lying dormant in my memory and adding them to my narrative.

The first pictures that I would point out were of two special employees; Sam Townsley and Frank McDonald.

In early 2000, Sam Townsley was our bell captain and had worked at the hotel for almost 50 years. When Sam came to the hotel in the 1950's, he was employed as one of the 125 waiters. Later on, Sam was put in charge of the bell stand. He had worked from the time he was 12, delivering newspapers, then at a B.F. Goodrich plant. Sam served in the Navy during World War II, and then got his degree in history and government with a minor in sociology from Kentucky State University. Later he was called up from the reserves during the Korean War, leaving his job at the hotel for two years. Mr. Sam was the best know man at the hotel, also in the town, the county, maybe in the state. Everyone knew and loved Sam Townsley. Sam didn't own or drive a car and he lived at the hotel. Johnny would sometimes drive Sam wherever he needed to go or he would ask Sam to go with him on outings. Johnny said that everywhere they went there was always someone who knew Sam. One day Sam went with Johnny to a music store in Vincennes, Indiana, and the owner's dad happened to be there. Sure enough, *that* man knew Sam. Sam Townsley was awarded the Lieutenant Governor's Hoosier Hospitality Award for Orange County in 2001, and no one could have deserved it more.

Frank McDonald had worked at the French Lick Springs Hotel from 1907 until 1968 and was chief engineer of the power plant for most of those years. Then when I would say, "And Frank McDonald was my father." I would always see a new level of interest come into the eyes of the guests. I learned early on that stories about the people who had played a part in the history of the hotel were often the favorite part of the tour.

chapter 6

My Family At The Hotel

One would be hard pressed to find a family in French Lick who did not have at least one member with a work history at the French Lick Springs Hotel. After the purchase of the hotel by Tom Taggart in 1901, the hotel grew into a small city that required porters, valets, maids, elevator operators, telephone and telegraph operators. There was a laundry that was equipped to handle a town of 20,000. There were shops that sold clothing, jewelry, tobacco and a newsstand. There was a broker's office, barber shop, beauty salon, bath attendants, doctor, chemist and photographer. There was a greenhouse, stable, dairy, vegetable garden, water treatment plant, and a power plant providing electricity and water to the hotel and the town. There were painters, paperhangers, carpenters, upholsterers, cooks, bakers, servers, musicians, office workers and managers.

The number of men employed at the golf courses included the grounds keepers who had to pull weeds from the greens by hand. There would be a line of twelve men and boys, moving together across each green as they pulled the weeds. Caddies were still in use in the 1950's when the hotel would ask the school for any boys who were available to leave school and serve as caddies.

This gives just a glance at the workforce required to operate the French Lick Springs Hotel.

Nearly everyone in my family has worked to the hotel at one time or another starting with my grandparents Maude and Bert Charnes, my parents Wava and Frank McDonald, my brother Tommie and half-brother Harold, daughter Julie and granddaughters Tabitha and Fawn, two of my mother's sisters and several of my mother's brothers. One of my mother's brothers worked for my father in the power plant. He told me that Daddy always whistled as he walked around the plant so that his men knew when he was approaching and were never caught being idle. Daddy was fiercely protective of the men who worked for him, not letting anyone outside the plant give orders to his men, and that included other supervisors such as convention managers and food and beverage managers.

My Father

When my father was born in 1891, the hotel had been around for over a half century as a health resort. But for my father's family, the hotel was of little consequence. From what I was able to glean from my father about his childhood I know his father, William Hugh McDonald, was a farmer, a circuit-riding Methodist Minister, and Constable. I got the impression that his mother, Martha Frances Shields, known as 'Mattie', was a kind but strict lady who insisted that her children must never play cards or go to dances, and on her death bed made them all promise that they would never belong to a lodge. This last edict came about because one of her sons had belonged to a lodge when he died and the money he had paid into the lodge for life insurance was never paid to the family. As far as I know, my father didn't play cards or dance but he never imposed those restrictions on anyone else in our home.

My father had started school in a one-room school house when he was four years old. His teacher would sometimes take him to school with her, on her horse. The children used a slate and chalk to do their writing and arithmetic. I have his slate that is actually two slates, bound together like a book. He learned to read using the McGuffey reader and the Indiana Educational Series of graded lesson books. I enjoy reading the books that I have of his, especially the fifth grade reader that has works of

Walter Scott, John Greenleaf Wittier, Lord Byron, William Shakespeare, Charles Dickens, Henry Wadsworth Longfellow, Oliver Wendell Holmes, Thomas Jefferson, Walt Whitman, Alfred Tennyson, Abraham Lincoln, Washington Irving and Victor Hugo. I find it remarkable that these young children were being introduced to such wonderful literature.

One day as we were driving through West Baden in our maroon colored 50' ford, he began telling me about when and why he had quit school.

Daddy said that on the first day of his sixth grade of school, there was a new teacher, a man, and he was hiding behind the door holding a stick. As each unsuspecting boy walked into the room the teacher hit the boy with the stick. Daddy said, "I caught on to what was happening and I turned around and never went back to school again." But his education didn't stop there. He went on to educate himself, reading and studying a variety of subjects including science, religion, mathematics and engineering.

As a young "drop-out", he sometimes worked at both of the hotels' bowling alleys as a pin setter. I remember seeing pin setters at a small bowling alley that I once visited in French Lick and I was fascinated by the agility these boys exhibited. The boys would perch above the pins and when the pins were knocked down the pin setter would jump down and quickly place the pins in a V shape contraption that he operated manually. When the pins were in place the pin setter lowered them to the alley for the next bowler.

These boys worked 12 hour shifts. The hotels paid them no wages so they were dependent on the tips that the guests gave them. Usually a pin setter would only get a penny or a nickel, depending on how quickly the boy replaced the pins and how generous was the guest. One day Daddy was setting pins at West Baden and after the game the man called him out and flipped him a silver dollar. Daddy had never received that much money at one time in his whole life.

With this big tip, Daddy could now afford the 5 cents fare to ride the streetcar to French Lick, the first leg of his journey home. But rather than break the silver dollar Daddy chose to walk all the way to his home that was beyond where the Donald Ross Golf Course is today. I have a feeling he was pretty proud to show his family that bright shiny dollar.

At the age of 15, my father began working part-time as a caddy at the French Lick Springs Hotel and on March 7, 1910 he started working full-time at the power house. His first job was shoveling coal.

One story I heard about my father took place early in his employment. The hotel needed someone to make sure the pump in one of the pump houses didn't stop running during any rain storm that might come up at night. They didn't want to have someone stay with the pump every night, just to be there if needed. Daddy volunteered. One night a dark, threatening cloud came blowing in over the hills. Daddy saw it and ran through the woods and down the hills for the two miles to the hotel's pump house from his home. When he got to the pump house the cloud just kept rolling on by and no rain fell. Daddy carefully slipped back home; he didn't want anyone to know that he had been on a 'fool's errand'. The next day when he got to work his boss said, "Frank, I put you in for an extra day's pay." Daddy asked, "Why?" and his boss said, "That cloud fooled me too."

This young man continued to prove himself and in 1915, at the age of 23, was promoted to chief engineer, holding that position until he retired on February 15, 1968, at the age of 76. That is a long time in the life of a man and a long time in the life of his family, or in my father's case, his two families.

When Frank McDonald became the chief engineer of the power house, he was married to his first wife, Cynthia. They would eventually become parents of four children. Their oldest, Harold, would join his father at the power house and eventually was named the chief electrician. All of his children were talented in music. Harold played and made guitars and banjos. His three daughters, Opal, Violet, and June, known as "The McDonald Sisters", sang throughout southern Indiana and also sang on the radio. Violet not only sang but also accompanied the trio on guitar. Sadly, their mother died when the youngest child was 16 and the sisters never sang together again.

Daddy was an organizer. He took his National Geographic magazines and compiled similar subject-matter into separate bound books. If I had to do a report at school on, say, Holland, all I had to do was go into our big walk-in closet that was attached to our bathroom and on the top shelf were the bound books he had put together. (On the first shelf, behind the washcloths was where he hid his bottle of Four Roses whisky). I just found the book about Holland and all the information was right there.

I remember a bookcase of his that sat in the dining room, beside the piano, that had many kinds of books on a variety of subjects. One book titled, *THE SUN, MOON, AND STARS* was a book Daddy used to try to teach me astronomy. He would point out different constellations and would sit with me on our front steps that faced north, to watch meteor showers. Daddy would get impatient with me because I could never remember how fast was the speed of light or how many light years the North Star was from earth. Don't look for the answers here because I still don't know. That is what Google is for. This was one of the first insights into my numerical deficiency. I'm not sure if that is an actual term but it fits me. I can only remember numbers if they are dates. I cannot remember numbers of distances and for the life of me I cannot remember a number with a dollar sign in front of it.

About a year after my father's first wife died, there was a pretty, young widow working in the laundry who caught his attention. Her name was Wava Charnes Wininger and she would become my mother.

Both Frank McDonald and Wava Charnes Wininger had very little leisure time; Frank worked Monday through Saturday and half a day on Sunday, and Wava, when away from the hotel, was taking care of her brothers and sisters at home. I doubt if my parents would have ever met had it not been for the hotel.

My Mother

Mother was the oldest of eleven children, one had died in infancy. Her mother, my grandmother, Maude Bell, had worked at the hotel as a telephone operator before she married my grandfather, Bert Charnes. My grandfather worked at the hotel as a painter and paperhanger and my mother, Wava, when she was around nine or ten would go to work with him and help him hang wallpaper. My grandmother died in January of 1932, at the age of 43 of a heart attack and my mother was widowed in March of that same year, just fifteen months after her first marriage. She and her first husband had no children so Mother went home to help care for her younger brothers and sisters. My grandfather died three years later, in November 1935, at the age of 50, of what was apparently congestive heart failure, leaving Mother with the full responsibility of the care of her younger siblings. The older boys worked as caddies at the hotel to help supply income to the family and my mother took a job at the hotel laundry. The laundry was situated next to the power plant and I like to imagine my father walking through the laundry and seeing this pretty, young widow and falling head over heels in love. I am such a romantic. They never told me how their courtship and subsequent marriage came about but I'm glad that Daddy dared to start a new family at the age of 46. They were married on January 6, 1937, and I was born on January 8, 1938. I was probably around four years old when I learned the dates of my parent's anniversary and my birthday. One summer day we went to a farm to buy fresh churned butter. I was fascinated with the churn as I saw how butter was made. The farmer was talking to my mother when he turned to me and asked, "How old are you?" I told him, "Four", and then felt the need to expound on the subject so I added, "My mother and daddy were married on January sixth and I was born on January eighth." My mother quickly chimed in, "A year later!" Do I really remember this? Oh, yes I do, and I never missed a chance to use it, just to watch my mother's reaction. She never failed me.

My father was twenty years my mother's senior but because of or in spite of that, age has never been of any importance to me.

By the time my parents married some of Mother's brothers and sisters were already on their own with only my Aunt Betty, age 13, Uncle Bill, age 10 and Uncle Duke, age 8, still at home. Aunt Betty came to live with Mother and Daddy. Uncle Bill and Uncle Duke went to live with their mother's sister Clara, who had a son close to their ages.

Chapter 1

Continuing The Tour

After the picture tour of the hotel's history we would encounter the two statues of Pluto standing sentinel in the lower regions of the hotel. These had once stood on top of the hotel's Pluto Bar but were removed because they were offensive to some convention groups. They had also frightened away some new employees who chose to return home rather than face Pluto.

When the present casino was first opened, Pluto stood at the entrance of the high-roller room but again had to be moved because some patrons felt that he was unlucky. They obviously were misinformed about Pluto. In Roman mythology, Pluto was a distributor of wealth to deserving people, thus a *plutocrat* is a wealthy and influential person.

Most guests just looked at the Pluto statues as a good place to have their picture taken.

The Convention Hall

As the tour group moved along we would go the Grand Colonnade Ballroom which was part of the 1924 addition. Originally known as The Convention Hall, this and the meeting rooms on the floor above were added to accommodate the ever increasing demand for convention services.

During a convention of Democrat Governors in 1932, Franklin Delano Roosevelt, then Governor of New York, and Mrs. Eleanor Roosevelt were among the distinguished guests. It was at this convention that FDR gained the support he sought from fellow Governors as he prepared to throw his hat in the ring for the Presidency of the United States of America in 1933.

The Garden

When weather permitted I would take guests out to the garden where the guests had a better vantage point to grasp the true size of the hotel.

As I stood with my back to the pond I would face the tour group and point out that we were standing where the Pavilion had been. Built in 1888, new owners endeavored to turn the French Lick Hotel into a first-class hotel. The Pavilion added a place for recreation with a bowling alley, billiard tables, a dance floor, and, on the second floor there was a casino.

On the far side of the garden where now is the Convention Center, there had been a small hill with steps made out of flat rocks leading up to the top of the rise where water trickled down to the pond below. An old walnut tree stood atop the little hill.

One day in mid-autumn I was speaking to a large group who had come to the hotel by tour bus. I was zoned-in on my talk, barely aware of a noise that sounded like a "plop, plop," in the water behind me. Then I noticed that smiles were appearing on the faces of my group; then giggles; then they all started laughing out loud. My first thought was, "Oh, my gosh, what did I say?", but when I turned around I saw a very determined squirrel high up in the walnut tree throwing walnuts into the pond below. "Plop, Plop, Plop". I had been upstaged by a squirrel.

The garden had once been called The Japanese Garden but after the bombing of Pearl Harbor, it was called the Oriental Gardens. The name 'Japanese' wasn't very popular at that time.

There are two tall Japanese ginkgo trees in the garden. These trees are a symbol of longevity, being able to live for a 1,000 years. They have survived earthquake and fire. Many of these trees even survived the atomic bomb that was dropped on Hiroshima on August 6, 1945. There are around 170 of those trees, now called "A-bombed trees," still living in Japan today. Thankfully the two trees in the French Lick Springs Hotel's garden were preserved when the garden underwent a major reconfiguration in 2006.

Pluto and Proserpine

There had been another mineral spring just east of the large Pluto spring, and it was called by the name of Pluto's wife, Proserpine or Proserpina. If I may be allowed to paraphrase the story, I tell it like this:

"It seems that Pluto was feeling the yen to have a wife but there wasn't much to choose from where he lived. He also wasn't known for his good looks. So with his usual savoir-faire, Pluto just kidnapped Proserpine, the beautiful daughter of Demetra, the goddess of the earth, and took her to his underground home.

"Well, Demetra was so sad with the abduction of her beautiful daughter that she went into a depression, just as many mortal mothers do when their precious daughters get married, and the sadder she became, the colder the earth became until it was winter all year. 'If momma isn't happy, nobody is happy'.

"Zeus interceded and convinced Pluto to let Proserpine go home to visit her mother for part of the year which made Demetra happy, bringing forth spring until the full warmth of summer. But when daughter Proserpine had to return to Pluto, mamma got depresses again and the weather began to grow colder, causing the four seasons on the earth every a year. However, if you live in the Midwest, you might have four seasons in one day."

The Pluto Spring

My favorite part of the tour was at the Pluto spring. I know that was not the favorite place for some guests who had very sensitive olfactory nerves; they were the ones who stayed a great distance from the spring. But the ones who dared to come down and stand around or sit on the small ledge that surrounded the spring got to hear the story.

At the spring one discovers that the reason for this hotel is right under your nose. While some folks might smell this water and think of rotten-eggs, Doctor William Bowles smelled money.

Doctor William Bowles, a physician from Paoli built the first house on this land to accommodate his patience. According to an advertisement that he placed in a newspaper in June 1855, the waters were useful for the treatment for everything from indigestion to emotional instability to skin diseases. Of course these claims were excessive but the mineral water DID have many helpful qualities, chief among these was its colon cleansing ability.

Today the spring that was accessible for over a century and a half is no longer accessible due to the wall that surrounds it. For the first time in its long history, people think it is a wishing well and throw coins into it. Prior to the "wall" sometimes an adventuresome guest would bring a water bottle or cup on the tour and take a taste of the Pluto water from the spring. I once saw a guest carrying jugs, and I mean at least four of those gallon milk jugs, full of Pluto water he had collected from the spring to take back home. Not sure if they were for personal use or for a friend (or for an enemy), but he was loaded for bear.

When I was a young girl my father took me to Pluto's spring and showed me how to drink the water. There were glass goblets attached to long wooded handles sitting on the ledge behind the spring. Daddy took one of the goblets, rinsed it out in the overflow, dipped the goblet in the spring and gave me a taste. The water was very cold, salty and tasted of minerals. I remember that the taste was not offensive, just different.

In the early part of the 20th century, there was sometimes a person, usually one of the waiters, dressed as Pluto who would serve the guests the Pluto water. But most often guests would serve themselves. After a good stiff drink the guest would pick up a cane that was available in the spring house and then take a walk around the third of a mile circular pathway beyond the spring. Outhouses were strategically placed around the path and if a cane was hanging outside an outhouse door that signaled that the outhouse was occupied, necessitating a quick jaunt to the next available outhouse. You see, this was the Victorian era and it was considered rude to knock on an outhouse door. I think it was at French Lick that "Jogging" may have been invented.

Sam Townsley told me that when he came to work at the hotel in the 1950's one of his duties was to place a jug of hot Pluto water outside the door of every guest room. This practice had been in place since 1901 to ensure that guests could greet each new day with a real "Eye-opener".

Pluto water was also piped directly up to the Pluto Bar where cold or hot Pluto water was accessible in all kinds of weather. The Pluto Bar was located where the 1875 Steak House is now.

Pluto water was piped into the spa, allowing guests to enjoy the benefits of a Pluto bath. I have taken the Pluto bath and found it to be both relaxing and invigorating. To me, there is much more to it than just a nice warm soak in the tub.

Pluto Travels the World

A new bottling plant was built across the street from the hotel in 1913 and "Pluto" became a household word. If you couldn't come to French Lick, French Lick could come to you. Pluto Water could be purchased at any drugstore in the land. These bottles were shipped all over the United States, even traveling to other countries as was confirmed by a guest on one of the history tours. She said, "When I was in Nova Scotia at the Maritime Museum I saw menus from all the ships that made port there in the early part of the 20th century and every menu offered Pluto Water."

Not only did these little bottles with the recognizable picture of Pluto as a Red Devil serve as a remedy for "what ails you" but they were advertising the French Lick Springs Hotel in the process.

~

The fresh water spring has beautiful rock ledges that made it a popular background for photographs. One day a gentleman approached my desk with a picture of his grandfather and his grandfather's new bride. The picture was taken prior to 1901, and the gentleman was wondering if I could identify where the picture had been taken. I recognized immediately that they were at the fresh water spring with the rock wall behind them. I then took him to the very spot where his grandfather had once stood holding in one hand a glass water goblet that was attached to a wooden handle and in the other hand he was holding a cane, the kind that was provided for walking the track. I remembered using the same type of goblet when I had my first taste from the Pluto Spring.

Chapter 8

Front, Back And Heart Of The House

In the hotel business, the term 'Front of the House' refers to the part of the hotel that guests' see and 'Back of the House' is what guests don't see, like the kitchen and laundry. But there is a part of the hotel that I consider the 'Heart of the House'.

Until I was 20 years old I had never walked up the impressive front steps nor entered through the front door to the lobby, but rather I had often walked past the coal cars and through the power plant door to the engine rooms.

I had never seen the mosaic tile floor or beautiful pillars that adorned the lobby, but I had seen the cement floor where my father's wonderful roll top desk with all the pigeonholes and the swivel chair sat in the first engine room that served as my father's office.

I had never seen the marble stairs that led from one floor to another in the hotel but I had seen the marble wall in the engine room with all the levers and gages that looked like clocks to me.

I had never seen the crisp, white uniforms of the waiters but I had seen the coal dust on the men who shoveled coal into the boilers that generated the steam heat to the entire hotel property.

I saw the work-stained clothes of painters and carpenters who kept the hotel's heart beating long before I saw the elegance and opulence that was seen by our guests as the French Lick Springs Hotel.

But before I had ever seen any of this I had heard the noon whistle.

The Noon Whistle

As soon as I heard that whistle I knew that my father would soon be parking his car in front of our home and we would be eating our noon dinner. Our dog, Punkie, also knew that whistle meant that his master would be home soon and always took up his post at the front of our house to wait for my father.

That same whistle blew sometimes at night and that meant that everyone had to close all window curtains and extinguish any outside lights. All street lights were turned off and if you were in a car you had to pull over, turn off your headlights and prepare to take cover if we were attacked. This was a world at war.

During World War II, every city and town in the United States had air-raid drills at night to prepare us in the event of an attack by enemy air planes. Air-raid wardens, local men, patrolled the streets to make sure no lights were visible because the smallest light, even the lighting of a cigarette outside, could be seen from the air. When the air-raid wardens finished checking, the hotel whistle would sound the "all clear" so street lights and house lights were allowed back on.

I was only one year old when Hitler invaded Poland in September 1939 and just one month shy of my fourth birthday when the Japanese bombed Pearl Harbor, so my earliest memories are of a world at war; men and women in uniform, people being sad because someone they loved had 'gone off to war', flags in windows with a star on the flag representing family members who were in the service, and if there was a gold star, that meant that someone was never coming back home.

Several of my mother's brothers wore army uniforms and her cousins wore navy blue. My uncle Alvia and some of his army buddies would send me chewing gum that they bought at the PX and one Christmas he sent me a little doll named "Tookie". My uncle Wayne was also in the army and one time he brought an army buddie, Jerome Sandusky, to our house when they were on leave. That was the first time I fell in love. You never forget your first love even if you are only three years old.

The first songs I remember are songs that Aunt Betty taught me; silly songs like "Mairzy Doats", "Three Little Fishies", "A Tisket A Tasket" and sad songs like "The White Cliffs of Dover". Even though I was a little girl, "The White Cliffs of Dover" made me sad because I understood the words were about a little boy, a child like me, who was not in his home because of the war.

On the home front, everyone was participating in the war effort. Women who had never worked outside the home were now working in factories, helping fill the place of our men who were fighting in the service of our country. Women were flying airplanes from the factories to military air bases and serving in great numbers in the military. At our house, we did as families all across the United States were doing. We saved tin foil, even the small amount that chewing gum was wrapped in, and recycled anything that could be used in the war effort; in fact, we invented recycling. We had books with stamps that we had to turn in whenever we made a purchase of gasoline, sugar, or anything that was rationed and that was most everything. New cars were not being built but Jeeps were, along with tanks, airplanes, battle ships, etc. Families grew what was called "Victory Gardens". We grew as much food as possible for our own consumption. I even had my own little "Victory Garden" where I grew radishes, onions, and leaf lettuce. We all bought war bonds, lending money to the war effort to be paid back years into the future. I had a little Women's Army Corp uniform complete with a WAC style purse.

One day my mother got a letter from her brother Wayne, where he told her that he and some of his unit had found some chickens in an abandoned farm house somewhere in Europe and how excited they were to be able to eat fresh cooked meat. We were just about to sit down to a meal and Mother was so upset, thinking of what her brothers must be going through that she cried and couldn't eat. Today we laugh and joke about our parents telling us to "Clean your plate. There are children who are going hungry in other parts of the world." But, I didn't think it was so funny then. I worried about all those children. Of course, what we are laughing about is not the poverty of others but the absurdity of our eating our food helping alleviating someone else's need. (I was raised on guilt.) It was scary to enter this world under such a dark cloud as a World War but I knew that my uncles and other young men were out there protecting me and our home and that gave me a safe feeling. Nevertheless, I remember having nightmares, I suppose all children have them, but mine were that Nazi soldiers were in my yard.

I remember V-E Day, May 8, 1945, when the war in Europe ended and V-J Day, August 15, 1945 when the war with Japan ended and everyone in French Lick went to their respective church to give thanks that the war was finally over and our loved ones would soon be coming home.

Everyone in our family came home but none came home unharmed. My uncle Alvia carried a bullet in his chest for the remainder of his life from being wounded in battle, Uncle Wayne had ulcers that cost him half of his stomach and all who did come home carried scars, some visible and some that could not be seen but nevertheless were there. Post-traumatic stress, or PTS, wasn't yet in our vocabulary but the results of war were heavy in the minds of the returning veterans. Uncle Alvia could never speak of the war nor could he see a movie about the war, so deep were the wounds he carried. These men and women are now called "the greatest generation" but even as a child I knew that they were the greatest.

Social Media

Before the advent of the cell phone we had our own form of social-media; facetime was really face-to-face time; in place of a text, written letters were sent and often saved and treasured; and we never had to look for our phones.

We also had a local newspaper. Once a week we could read about who was visiting whom, who went to the hospital, and with no HIPAA, we could all know what so-in-so was being treated for, or died from. We knew who was home and who was not home; making "neighborhood watch" a way of life.

When the power plant whistle sounded at some time other than the usual noon whistle, it was a signal that an emergency had struck the hotel or town, such as a fire. To find out what had happened we just called the telephone operator and she would spread the news.

The telephone office was located behind the bank that was on the corner of maple and college streets, just half a block from the main part of town. The telephone operator was the information center of French Lick, sort of a one-woman social media app. At one of our French Lick High School Alumni Banquets, a former classmate related to me a funny thing that happened back in the 1950's. She had called the telephone operator and asked her to ring "1-2-3", which was my phone number. The operator said, "Eva Sharron isn't home. I just saw her and her mother walk past the telephone building."

If you thought Andy Griffith's "Mayberry" phone service was stretching it a bit, you should have lived in French Lick. As in "Mayberry", party lines were common and if you were lucky enough to have one you could listen in on other people's conversations. I wasn't so lucky. We had a private line because of my father's position at the hotel.

When the phone rang in the middle of the night at our house, we knew that was not a good thing. Those late night phone calls usually signaled an emergency at the hotel. Daddy would quickly dress, pulling his trousers on over his pajama pants, pajama top serving as his shirt, his leather romeo house slippers for shoes, grab a jacket and out the door… boy, could he move fast. As Chief Engineer of the Power Plant, Daddy was responsible for all of the energy that was generated for the hotel: guest rooms, spas that were referred to as "Men's and Women's Baths", bowling alleys, dining rooms, meeting rooms and barber shop, plus the dairy, horse stables, 2 golf courses, skeet club, waiters' quarters and the Taggart residence.

Sometimes there might be a dispute at night among the personnel and Daddy would be called in to negotiate a truce. I can only imagine the "negotiation" part and well imagine the language used. Daddy could scare the pants right off you. One time when the local "supreme keeper of the white race" (my title) was on the hotel's property, threatening the black employees, Daddy was called and as he prepared to leave the house I won't even begin to repeat what he said when he got THAT call. (But my brother can repeat every #*!%#!* that was uttered.)

Chapter 9

A Road Through
The Wilderness

It was a hot, humid day in French Lick when a lady came staggering up to me, put her hands on my desk to steady herself, and with red face and wilting hair asked, (it was more an accusation than a question), "Who built that road, some *Animal?*"

Well, it had always been obvious to me that the roads had to be curvy because of the hills, but I had never given much thought as to who had built the roads. But right then and there I felt the facts that I had been learning as I delved into the history of the area start spinning around in my head and suddenly they fell into place and I answered,

"Yes."

The road to French Lick was actually "built" by American bison, commonly called "buffalo". As these animals migrated from the western Plains of Illinois, to the Big Bone Lick in Boone County, Kentucky, they would go a little bit out of their way to visit the salt lick in this valley where the mineral water was flowing freely and leaving a salty residue on the rocks. The buffalo would lick the rocks and wallow in the swampy earth surrounding the lick. It was said that as many as 500 hundred buffalo, sometimes 20 to 30 abreast and taking up to three days to pass, would be seen in a single herd, packing the soil into hard roads. There is a story about a steamboat Captain who said that he saw so many buffalos crossing the Ohio River at one time that they blocked the river for miles. These migrations continued until around the year 1800.

This Buffalo Trace had many "firsts":

1. the first road surveyed and opened in Indiana,
2. the first mail route in Indiana,
3. the first road built by State funds in Indiana,
4. the first Stage line in Indiana,
5. the first Toll road in Indiana.

It is now a state highway that passes in front of the French Lick Resort, namely State Highway 56.

Early travelers most often moved westward following waterways that offered a "path of least resistance", but a "beaten path" that stretched from the falls of the Ohio River to the falls of the Wabash River, offered a means for overland travel to pioneers and to armies.

Next Question: Why is this place called French Lick?

Well, the answer to that question is tied to the answer of the previous question. Passersby who were traveling the Buffalo Trace called this spot by various names: "The Lick" was the most common name; other names were, "The Great Salt Lick" and "The Buffalo Lick". No matter what they called it, the name "lick" was always included. I found a diary written by John Parsons of Virginia during a trip through Indiana that he made following his graduation in 1839 from the University of Virginia. He states that he regretted that he didn't have the time to visit a place called *the French Lick*.

We really aren't certain where the name "French" came from. Of course, Indiana was within the province of Louisiana and under French control in the early 1700's.

The 'go to' explanation is that the French had a fort here at some time and that French fur traders may have visited this area but I am not altogether satisfied with that answer. We do know that Vincennes, Indiana, the oldest town in Indiana, was first settled in 1732 as a French trading post for the trading of Buffalo hides, but as to the French coming down the Buffalo Trace to "The Lick" we really have no proof. In fact the French presence would have ended around 1763 and the first mention of a "fort" was not until 1807 when settlers were ordered to build "forts" or "blockhouses" to be used as military stations for the Rangers who patrolled the frontier and for settlers to sleep in at night as protection from the Indians.

There may have been more, but I have learned about only one casualty in French Lick at that time; a man named William Charles. Charles, a husband and father, had in some way offended the Indians living near the Lick. One day Charles was plowing his field that was in the vicinity where French Lick's Melton Library now stands when the Indians attacked and killed Charles. The shots fired attracted the attention of the soldiers who were at the fort and they rushed to Charles' field, arriving just in time to interrupt the scalping of William Charles. His body was buried near the fort and legend has it that the hotel is over the grave. Could be. The hotel covers a lot of ground.

The first time we find the name "French Lick" was in 1786 when General George Rogers Clark and his nearly 1000 men of the Kentucky Militia camped on these grounds on their way to Vincennes. Ironically, these troops whose mission was to help quiet the unrest that still plagued the western front began displaying their own discord upon meeting at the Falls of the Ohio that summer. This friction only intensified until an incident over a horse erupted and guns were fired in defiance of an order. This act of insubordination was recorded by a Captain Gaines, stating that this took place "at a place called French Lick". It seems that General Clark may have called it by that name because it reminded him of property he had once owned. In a letter to Patrick Henry, dated March 9, 1779, Clark mentions that he is in danger of losing land that he purchased in Tennessee on the Cumberland River at a place known as the great *French lick*.

At this point in my history tour, I would ask the group, "Have any of you ever heard of French Lick, Tennessee?" I would usually be met with blank looks and head shaking. On day I was leading a large group who had arrived on a bus tour and when I asked that question a little lady piped up and said, "I never even heard of *French Lick, Indiana.*" Sometimes I felt like a straight-man in a comedy act. But I continued to ask that question and was rewarded one day when a man said, "Yes, I know right where it is. There is a park where we play baseball that has a sign indicating where 'French Lick' was." By-the-way, that area is now called Nashville, Tennessee.

Initially the Buffalo Trace had been accommodating travelers who for many years were just passing through the Indiana Territory, but between 1810 and 1815 it began bringing people who wanted to stay; to start new lives and build new communities. The number of settlers began increasing until the population was well over the 60,000 minimum required for statehood. In 1811, a group of settlers, mostly Quakers from Orange County in north central North Carolina, moved to an area that they named Paoli. On December 11, 1816 Indiana became the nineteenth state to be admitted to the Union.

The big attraction at the springs at the French Lick originally was the salt for both animals and man. Salt was vital not only for flavoring but for preserving food. It was taken for granted that the French Lick would be a source of large quantities of salt, so houses were being erected all along the road between Jeffersonville and Vincennes. Early travelers would have found Inns or Taverns all along the way. These places for lodging had to follow certain laws; they must have at least one extra room, even though most travelers slept on the floor, and one extra stall.

The Enabling Act of April, 1816, granted the people of the Indiana Territory to form a constitution and state government, and for the admission of such state into the Union on an equal footing with the original states. It also granted thirty-six sections of land to the state for the manufacturing of salt. These saline reserves were under the control of the state and included the land around the French Lick springs. The method for extracting salt from the spring water was to boil the mineral water in large kettles causing the water to evaporate, leaving behind the salt. When that proved impractical, they tried boring to reach the water deeper in the ground, reasoning that the deeper water might have a higher content of salt. Not so. The salt content of the French Lick springs water just was not large enough to warrant all of the effort it took to manufacture the salt.

When the State of Indiana finally concluded that the saline reserve at French Lick was not going to supply adequate amounts of salt, Congress granted approval for the sale of the land. The land was to be sold at public auction at a minimum of $1.25 per acre. Thomas C. Bowles purchased some of the saline lands and then transferred them to his son, Doctor William Bowles around 1833.

chapter 10

Doctor William Bowles

Doctor William Bowles, a physician from Paoli, Indiana, was the first person to see the possible value of a hotel on these premises; a place where his patients could stay while using the mineral water for the improvement of their health.

Mineral Springs Resorts were beginning to be accepted in other parts of Indiana and in other states as well. We have no photographs of the very first building but later pictures of additions and improvements help us get a pretty good idea about the original building. A description by Mr. A. J. Rhodes, written in his little book, *EARLY HISTORY of WEST BADEN and FRENCH LICK SPRINGS and LOST RIVER*, that was written around 1904, gives his first impression of Doctor Bowles' Hotel when he was a young boy. Mr. Rhodes said the building was perhaps 80 to 100 feet long, was narrow and three stories.

Another building had two stories and extended some 40 feet to the south of the first building. Mr. Rhodes went on to say that the style of the building was to him "peculiar" and he even went so far as to say "it was the ugliest and most unsightly building ever constructed in the valley". Looking at actual photographs of the hotel taken before the fire destroyed the first hotel building in 1887, it appears that the original hotel faced north with the mineral springs in full view of the front of the original building. The hotel was on or near the site where the fort or blockhouse once stood.

Mr. Rhodes described Doctor Bowles, who was a friend of his father and the Rhodes family's physician, in most flattering detail. Rhodes said that Doctor Bowles was six-feet two-inches, weighed over 200 pounds, had a pleasant smile, a pleasing voice, and was self-confident and intelligent. Perhaps 'charismatic' would be a word we might use to describe him.

A newspaper in Paoli reported that on the Fourth of July, 1845, a celebration was held at Doctor Bowles' new building at the French Lick. This is the first mention of the French Lick hotel. I find it interesting, if not relative to this narrative, that Henry David Thoreau moved into his cabin near Walden Pond on that same day.

Doctor Bowles was not only a physician; he was involved in many diverse activities, mostly in the Paoli area, that may have kept him from developing the Hotel at the French Lick for a decade after he became the owner. He was a member of the Indiana House of Representatives, a minister in the General Baptist Church, and a Colonel in the Mexican War. This latter "achievement" turned out to be one of the two major mistakes in his life.

When war was declared against Mexico on May 13, 1846, concerning the annexation of Texas to the United States, the Secretary of War called for the Governor of Indiana to furnish three regiments of volunteers. They were to rendezvous at Camp Clark, (today's Clarksville). Among the volunteers was Doctor William Bowles. Three of my own ancestors, brothers Elihu (my great-grandfather), Eli, and David Jones McDonald were among the 5,000 volunteers from Indiana. The presence of both the Governor and Lieutenant Governor who were Democrats seems to have influenced the volunteers to vote for officers along party lines because all officers were Democrats. One of the colonels elected was William A. Bowles.

In October that same year, Doctor Bowles left his Regiment in Mexico and returned to French Lick and didn't return to Mexico until January of 1847. While he was gone, supposedly due to ill health, the Indiana Troops were placed under General Zachary Taylor.

Doctor Bowles' ineptitude as a colonel may have contributed to a terrible incident that happened near Buena Vista on February 23, 1847, bringing disgrace to the Indiana Second Regiment of volunteers.

Confusion or Cowardice?

On February 21st, General Santa Ana began advancing toward the United States troops. The next day, February 22nd, General Santa Ana's 20,000 soldiers confronted the 5,000 volunteers from Indiana. At dawn on the 23rd, the battle began again with two Mexican divisions of 7,000 men facing the 360 men of the Indiana Second Regiment. The Indiana Second Regiment held their ground, firing 20 rounds of ammunition. As the battle raged on the number of casualties on both side increased. It was on that day at the battle of Buena Vista that my great-great uncle, David Jones McDonald fell mortally wounded.

General Joseph Lane commanding the left side of the Indiana line decided to move forward and at the same time Colonel Bowles ordered his company to cease fire and retreat. Confusion ensued and men didn't know which way to go. When Bowles realized the mistake he had made he gathered as many of his men as he could and they joined the Mississippi troops under the command of Jefferson Davis.

When Bowles and the local veterans returned home they were given a hero's welcome at French Lick, complete with food, music and speeches. Bowles was riding high but was soon to fall hard when the full news of the Battle at Buena Vista reached home.

Although the Americans won the war, the dispute over the retreat of the Indiana troops went on for years. Eventually Bowles requested a court of inquiry for himself. The court found that Bowles had not lacked personal courage but that he did lack the capacity and judgement as a commander. Zachary Taylor laid the blame for the retreat on the Indiana volunteers. In spite of the court's findings General Lane put the entire blame on Bowles. This controversy was never completely settled in the minds of all concerned, resulting in a loss of respect for Doctor Bowles and leaving a dark cloud of cowardice hovering over the Indiana volunteers.

Dr. William Sherrod who had served in Buena Vista had an argument with Doctor Bowles at the Paoli post office in October of 1849. Doctor Sherrod drew and fired a pistol but no one was hurt. That incident didn't sound plausible to me, the part about no one being hurt, until I was reminded of something my brother had told me about our father.

It seems that Daddy, from around the age of 12, was well known as a bright young man who was handy at fixing guns. Often people gave him their guns to repair or to improve upon. Daddy told how black powder weapons, which would have been in use at that time, were less powerful than the later smokeless gunpowder weapons. He said two men could stand and shoot at each other all day and never hit their adversary. If they did happen to hit the other person, the impact of the bullet was such that often a heavy jacket could repel the lead.

But this climate of disrespect was very foreign to Doctor Bowles and soon after the incident with Doctor Sherrod, Bowles moved to a house in French Lick that he had recently built on the hillside facing the springs.

~

While Bowles was away in Mexico, he leased the French Lick Hotel to a Doctor John A. Lane. Doctor Lane was not a physician but a patent medicine peddler. Under his management the French Lick Hotel began to prosper. Besides the mineral water, the hotel was becoming a place for meetings, dances, and various public activities. Seeing the potential for hotels connected with mineral springs, Doctor Lane purchased some land that had mineral springs a mile north of French Lick. After Doctor Bowles returned to French Lick and resumed the operation of the French Lick Springs Hotel, Doctor Lane just went a mile up the road and built his own hotel. It was called Mile Lick Inn….because it was a mile from The Lick. Now we had competition.

The resorts at Mile Lick and French Lick were thriving as were the other five mineral spring resorts in Indiana. At French Lick, Dr. Bowles advertised the wonders of the mineral water for relieving and curing chronic ailments of the stomach, liver, spleen, kidneys, and skin besides being beneficial for the lame and infirmed. He also claimed the waters could prevent diseases of the lungs. Bowles built the first bath house and, in 1851, was selling mineral water by the barrel.

The saying, "You can't get there from here." probably originated with folks asking directions to the French Lick/West Baden Springs valley. You don't just happen to come *through* French Lick, you have to come here *on purpose.* In the 1850's the nearest railroad station was at Orleans, Indiana. Doctor Bowles helped solve the problem of transportation for guests by making available carriages to carry guests to and from the railroad station at Orleans.

In 1857, Dr. Bowles was instrumental in platting the town of French Lick. This was the beginning of the close relationship between the town and the hotel that has continued through the years.

In the early 1800's pioneers moving westward through Ohio and Indiana started getting sick from what was commonly called "milk sickness". The Thomas Lincoln family had moved from Kentucky to southern Indiana in December 1816, at the same time that Indiana achieved statehood. In the fall of 1818, Nancy Hanks Lincoln died of the milk sickness, leaving behind her husband and her children; nine year old Abraham and his eleven year old sister Sarah.

Doctor Bowles had been working on the cause and cure of milk sickness that we now know was caused by drinking the milk of cows that had eaten the white snakeroot. Doctor Bowles had hoped to publish his discoveries but apparently he allowed other matters to draw his attention away from his medical practice. This may have led to his ultimate downfall.

Slavery in Indiana

It was during this time in our country's history that sectionalism over slavery was spreading in the United States. Southern Indiana was largely Democratic and not altogether friendly towards the Abolitionist Movement. That is not to say that southern Indiana was in total agreement with pro-slavery, far from it.

After losing his brother in the Mexican War at Buena Vista, Great-Grandfather, Elihu, must have had his fill of war because he joined the Society of Friends and became a Quaker. Many people, including the Quakers, were actively opposed to slavery of anyone and were a part of the 'underground railroad'.

I have been told that some of the Quakers of Orange County would build their homes in a circle in order to place a wall of safety around slaves leaving Louisville and making their way north to freedom. I was also told that there was a place in Orange County near Paoli that was called 'Little Africa', where slaves could rest and find help before moving on to the next place of safety.

Doctor Bowles has received a lot of "bad press" by some historians because of his involvement in the Mexican War but none so much as his involvement with the Knights of the Golden Circle, a secret organization that grew up in the south and became anti-Lincoln, anti "Black" Republicans and pro-Confederate.

In 1857, French Lick made the newspapers as far away as the *New York Tribune* where the headline read, "Slavery in Indiana". The newspaper reported that Doctor Bowles had brought seven of his wife's slaves to French Lick. This was after the United States Supreme Court had decided that Dred Scott, a slave who had been living in two free states, could not sue for his freedom because he was not considered a person but property. (typing those words made me sick to my stomach) Besides blaming his wife, saying they were her slaves, not his, he was quoted as saying that they were in French Lick for their health. Seriously?

After two months his wife and her slaves returned to Louisville, Kentucky, and Bowles took the charge against him to the Indiana Supreme Court where the Court decided it was no penal offense because Dr. Bowles did not encourage them to remain in Indiana as slaves.

As a pro-southerner, the husband of a southern woman who owned slaves, and a strong Democrat, Bowles became more and more radical in his opposition to the union cause. He became a major-general in the Knights of the Golden Circle. In 1863 the name or the organization was changed to Order of American Knights but, no matter what name it was called, it was still pro-slavery.

According to a report given to the Governor of Indiana, Oliver Perry Morton, there were 40,000 members of the Knights of the Golden Circle in Indiana. Governor Morton, a Republican, was one of Lincoln's "war governors". He went to great lengths to quash treason and uphold the cause of the Union even to the point of exceeding his constitutional authority by suppressing the Democrat controlled state legislature, privately funding the state government, and calling out the state militia without approval.

Orange County was believed to be teeming with silent southern sympathizers, however when General John Hunt Morgan came to Indiana to rally men to the confederate cause, he got an unexpected welcome. The approach of Morgan's raiders was detected and citizens were apprised of their coming. Even my great-grandmother McDonald heard the warning and took all of her children to hide in their corn field. The Paoli newspaper, *The American Eagle*, reported in its July 2, 1863 edition that some of the raiders were captured within one mile of Paoli and the rest were run out of Orange County by 300 men.

Governor Morton once complained that Indiana had the most southern sympathizes of any free state. Nevertheless, Indiana supplied about 210,000 volunteers to the union forces. I am very proud to say that I had ancestors from Indiana of the McDonald family, and ancestors from Missouri of the Charnes family who fought in the Union Army during the Civil War.

~

A secret agent, Felix Stidger, a former union soldier, became a confidant of Bowles and infiltrated the Knights. He reported his findings to Brigadier-General Henry B. Carrington who commanded the district of Indiana, giving him a strong case against Bowles. On August 23, 1864, Bowles was arrested at his home in French Lick. At the end of their trial, Bowles, along with Lambden P. Milligan of Huntington, Indiana, and Stephen Horsey of Shoals, Indiana, were charged and found guilty of treason by a military commission and sentenced to death. Just three days before the execution was to take place, President Andrew Johnson intervened and later reduced the sentence to life imprisonment. This case went all the way to the Supreme Court of the United States resulting in the Ex Parte Milligan decision of April 5, 1866, that ruled the military commission had no jurisdiction as long as the civil courts were still functioning. So after serving 10 months in a prison in Columbus, Ohio, Bowles, Milligan, and Horsey were released.

The Ignoble End

Bowles returned to French Lick in 1866, a broken man, never able to live down the shame of being found a "traitor". In August of 1868, his wife, Eliza, filed for divorce. She had been his second wife; his first wife was deceased. Not long after being granted the divorce, Eliza died. Dr. Bowles then married his third wife, Julia, in April of 1872, and died March 28, 1873, at the age of 74. Now the grandchildren from his first marriage, the estate of his second wife and his widow were all vying for his estate that included the French Lick Hotel.

Before Bowles' arrest in August of 1864, the French Lick Hotel had been leased to Dr. Samuel Ryan, a young Doctor from Greenville, Indiana. This lease went into effect November 1, 1864, and was for fifteen years. Under Dr. Ryan's management the hotel continued to draw guests who were returning each year during "the season".

Chapter 11

Between Bowles And Taggart

Throughout the years of trying to establish just who were the rightful owners of the French Lick mineral springs and hotel, Doctor Samuel Ryan continued to manage and make improvements to the property.

In 1869, Doctor Joseph G. Rogers analyzed the waters at the three French Lick springs. He was impressed with the variety of minerals found in the springs and the curative abilities of the waters. His endorsement of the French Lick springs to other doctors was a boon to business. Dr. Rogers is the person responsible for the name "Pluto" being given to the largest spring at French Lick.

There seems to be differing accounts as to Pluto's role in mythology. One account says that Pluto was the ancient Roman deity of the dead, not responsible for their deaths but ruling over them once they were dead. Another account calls Pluto the god of wealth and lord of all the metals and riches that lie under the ground. I have no way of knowing what Dr. Rogers had in mind but the latter makes more sense to me. The minerals found in the water certainly have brought wealth to this valley.

Pluto's wife, Proserpine, had the second largest spring named for her. It was sometimes referred to as "the Beauty Spring".

The third and weakest spring was called Bowles Spring, named for Doctor Bowles.

In 1875, the hotel had bathing facilities, bowling alleys, croquet grounds, and a ballroom. The state geologist, E.T. Cox, visited the resort and reported that the hotel was well-built and well-ventilated.

Wells and Andrews

After eleven years of litigation, the hotel was finally sold to Doctor Samuel Ryan and local businessmen, Hiram E. Wells and James M. Andrews.

Sometime after 1880, Dr. Ryan sold his interest in the hotel to Wells and Andrews but remained the hotel's physician.

Wells and Andrews continued making improvements to the hotel that was welcoming more than 7,000 guests each year during the "watering season". In 1887, Wells bought out Andrews' interest and then turned right around and sold the property to a stock company from Louisville known as The French Lick Springs Company.

The French Lick Springs Company

The year 1888 saw the most improvements to the hotel property so far. That year the hotel boasted of having electric bells installed in all rooms along with the buildings and grounds being lighted with electricity and this being only nine years after the incandescent light bulb was invented by Edison. In 1888, the French Lick Springs Company granted a right of way for the Louisville, New Albany and Chicago Railroad and in 1889 a depot was built. By 1890, people could buy a round trip ticket to the springs at French Lick from any train station in Indiana, Illinois, Kentucky, and Ohio. The little valley with so many mineral springs was no longer isolated.

At the French Lick Springs a new building with guest rooms was built separate from the original building. This building was called "The Clifton" and the original building was now referred to as "The Windsor".

Room rates typically ran between $2 to $3.50 per day depending on the location of the room. This was during the time when a typical laborer in the United States would average around $14.50 in a 60 hour week.

Still another two-storied, wood frame building, "The Pavilion", was built facing the Windsor. The Pavilion had a dance floor and bowling alley on the first floor, and the second floor had a casino or card room.

So far, the hotel had only been open during the summer months, but when the yellow fever epidemic hit Jacksonville, Florida, in August of 1888, people began literally running for their lives from that popular winter resort city. The cause of this deadly disease, the bite of an infected mosquito, was at that time still unknown; what was known was that it struck warm, coastal regions and was a horrible illness that very often ended in death. People were urged to leave Jacksonville and those who did were most often coming north even though they had nowhere to stay. This influx of people needing accommodations may have influenced the French Lick Springs Company in their decision to start keeping the hotel open year-round for the first time in its history.

Dr. Ryan continued as resident doctor as the hotel added more employees including a hotel manager, a secretary, a barber, a photographer, and a band. Personally I am SO glad the French Lick Springs Hotel continued the practice of employing a band right through the Sheraton ownership, otherwise I would never have met my husband, Johnny Kobee.

The slow but sure prosperity enjoyed at the hotel resulted in more improvement being made. However, problems were looming on the horizon. The first came in August, 1897, when following a severe drought, the flow at Pluto and the other springs began to lessen until they stopped altogether in September. Without the mineral water the resort could not survive. Then on October 11, the Windsor burned, leaving only the Clifton to accommodate guests. But a few weeks later things started to look better for the resort. It was learned that the Windsor was sufficiently covered by insurance to not only rebuild but improvements to the Clifton could be made as well. When the drought ended the springs began to flow again though not as vigorously as they had. Before the drought the mineral water at the Pluto spring had a large amount of gas bubbles and as they would burst the popping noise could be heard far from the spring. There is a story of a German farmer and his son riding down the Buffalo Trace in a wagon in the early 1800's. As they came near "the lick" and smelled the sulfur and heard the explosions of the bubbles the father said, "Drive faster, John, Hell must be not half a mile from here!"

But after the drought Pluto no longer made the popping noise; I guess one might say that the drought had "burst Pluto's bubble". (*groan*)

Searching for Healthy Solutions

As the nineteenth century was drawing to a close, the number of mineral water resorts in Indiana had risen to 16 by 1890. That number almost doubled in the next ten years increasing to nearly 30 by 1900.

It is somewhat difficult for us today to imagine what it was like to live in this time period, especially when it comes to our health. This was a time when the life expectancy in the United States was 47. Heroin was available over the counter at drug stores and claimed by some to be "a perfect guardian of health". On May 8, 1886, Coca-Cola was first sold, and yes, it had cocaine in it. According to Wikipedia, it was invented by a Confederate Colonel, John Pemberton, who was wounded in the Civil War and became addicted to morphine. He began a quest to find a substitute for morphine. Coca-Cola was intended to be sold as a patent medicine and Pemberton claimed that Coca-Cola cured many diseases, including morphine addiction, indigestion, nerve disorders, headaches and impotence. In 1914, cocaine was removed from Coca-Cola.

People entering the 20th century were really no different from us today. They were looking for a safe and sure way to attain better health without harming themselves in the process. Mineral water flowing naturally from rocks in the earth only seemed logical.

While we may find it amusing to think that people would actually think that mineral water could have any health benefit…..wait a minute…. isn't that just exactly what many people ARE thinking? There is a mineral water on the market today that once even claimed the water was "Sexy". Of all the claims made by proponents of mineral water back-in-the-day, the one claim that I have NOT found was that the water was, by any stretch of the imagination, "Sexy". The main claim to fame of PLUTO water at French Lick was "The World's Greatest Laxative". One of the "new" things for better health today is to rid ourselves of things in our bodies that are actually making us sick. This sometimes requires "colon cleansing".

With the discovery of vitamins, first called "vitamine" in 1912 by Casimir Funk, he and other scientists began seeing how deficiencies of certain vitamins could contribute to certain illnesses.

In the 1920's multivitamins with minerals were said to increase appetite, aid digestion, correct constipation, clear the skin, give more energy and help put on weight.

Just as Doctors objected to the claims of mineral water, they also found the claims of the vitamin/mineral pills to be overstated.

I have suffered from Iron Deficiency Anemia or IDA, since I was first diagnosed at age four. I remember almost every detail of being taken to a specialist in Louisville. Daddy parked our car behind a Woolworth's five-and-dime store that was a block away from the doctor's office. I was too weak to walk so my father sat me on his arm and carried me up the street from the parking lot to the doctor's office. I was embarrassed because I thought I was too old to be carried. I was also embarrassed when I had to undress right down to my ruffled panties that my mother had made for me. A candy treat from a green dish that was shaped like a frog didn't do anything to endear me to those people who had humiliated me.

I was given some yucky tasting liquid that I had to take every day; I am assuming it contained vitamins and iron.

My IDA has plagued me all of my life and in the latter half of the 20th century I had some doctors tell me that taking vitamins and iron tablets just made expensive urine. But the truth is that with the help of Iron supplements I am able to control my anemia.

The Rest of the Story

I found a news release from an old newspaper that said when Paul Harvey was at the French Lick Hotel, he 'discovered' lithium in Pluto water and on his radio program, "The Rest of the Story", said that people were just being "drugged" into thinking they were healthier. In all of the chemical analysis of the springs, and after consulting with the manager of the Pluto Bottling Company, I learned that there is only a trace of lithium in the water and the decision to stop bottling the water was due to diminishing sales, nothing more…..and that is "The *True* Rest of the Story".

Chapter 12

Tom Taggart

During the 1890's, Tom Taggart and his family would sometimes visit the French Lick and West Baden hotels. Besides being prominent in state and national politics, Tom was also involved in the hospitality business as owner of the Depot Hotel and the Grand Hotel, both in Indianapolis. With a well-founded background in the hotel business, Tom could see a future in owning a mineral springs hotel in the French Lick/West Baden valley and began to visualize building his own hotel.

From Immigrant to Mayor of Indianapolis

Mayor Thomas Taggart was born in Amyvale, County Monaghan, Ireland, on November 17, 1856. His father, also named Tom, was born in Ireland in 1817. His mother, Martha Kingsbury Taggart, was born in Scotland in 1819. Tom had five sisters and one brother.

The family came to the USA in 1861, when young Tom was only five years old and settled in Xenia, Ohio, where his father got a job as baggage master at the Xenia railroad station. At twelve years old, Tom had to work half-days while going to school, cleaning the lunchroom floor at the Xenia depot, being sure to clean all the way into the corners. One day a lady told him that scrubbing floors was no excuse for not keeping a clean face. Tom took that to heart and carried that lesson with him throughout his life, even while he was poor, always looking clean and presentable.

Tom Taggart was a stickler for cleanliness. I heard it rumored that Mr. Taggart would sometimes hide money under a rug to reward employees for a thorough cleaning or perhaps to shame someone for just sweeping dirt under the rug.

By age sixteen he was promoted to working the lunch counter and after completing one year in high school, Tom began working full-time at the depot restaurant, leaving school behind.

In 1874, Tom became a United States Citizen and the next year his boss at the N. & G. Ohmer Company, sent him to Garrett, Indiana, to manage the De Kalb House, the depot hotel in that town. This young, likable Irishman was only eighteen years old.

While at Garrett, Tom met and fell in love with a young lady named Eva Bryant. This seems to have been a match written in the stars. Before the two had ever met a gypsy told Eva that she would marry a man whose initials were T. T. and they would have six children. On their first meeting Eva thought Tom was too kind and too polite to be anything but a fraud. But she soon learned that Tom Taggart was the real thing.

In 1877, Tom was again transferred this time to Indianapolis to work in the original Union Depot's restaurant. Tom and Eva were married the next year and as the gypsy predicted, they had six children; five girls and one boy: Florence Eva, Lucy Martha, Nora, Irene Mary, Thomas Douglas, and Emily Letitia.

Not Your Run-of-the-Mill Politician

Tom's personality was such that he simply enjoyed meeting people and making friends. The Union Depot was the hub of people from all walks of life and Tom's infectious personality attracted the attention of the men who were the leaders of the Democratic Party in Indianapolis. They encouraged

Taggart to run for public office so Tom began his political career as a precinct committeeman. In 1886 he was asked to run for Marion County Auditor. The chances of him winning were considered slim to none because Marion County was well known to be Republican. However, in the 1886 election, Tom Taggart won and began his four-year term in November, 1887. He went on to win reelection for the next term ending in 1891. In that reelection Tom's Republican opponent was a friend, so after defeating him, Tom paid all of that man's campaign expenses so his family would not suffer financially. Certainly, Tom Taggart was cut from a different cloth.

Tom Taggart continued to rise in Indianapolis politics all the way to being elected Mayor of Indianapolis for three successive terms from 1895-1901.

A Very Sad Time

In December, 1898, when Tom Taggart was in his second term as the mayor of Indianapolis his oldest daughter, twenty year old, Florence Eva, with some of her classmates from the St. Mary's Church Academy, went sailing on a yacht provided by the father of one of the young ladies, to Clearwater, Florida, where the young ladies planned to spend the winter. They set sail from Louisville, Kentucky, on December 6th and sailed down the Ohio River then down the Mississippi River to New Orleans. On January 3, 1899, the party again set sail from a lighthouse south of New Orleans in heavy fog and none on board was ever seen alive again. Their yacht had disappeared off the shores of New Orleans.

Tom Taggart left Indianapolis and went to New Orleans to direct the search for his daughter. A trunk was found by some fishermen on January 18th and the next day, Taggart identified the contents to be his daughter's. In May, her body was finally found on a sand strip called Grand Gosier Island, Louisiana, where it had been remarkably well preserved by white sand that had washed over her body by the gulf waves, serving as a grave, and had been hidden by a log. Tom Taggart thanked 'the Almighty for its deliverance". Hers was the only body ever recovered.

Half of the 57 ft. yacht was later found minus four feet where the gasoline tank had been that led to the conclusion that the cause of the accident may have been an explosion on board that split the vessel in half.

~

During this terrible time, Tom Taggart was facing the arduous task of running for Mayor for the third time. The Indianapolis Democrats were insistent that he run even if he might have chosen not to. He did run and he won, therefore serving his third and final term as the Mayor of Indianapolis. Not bad for a poor immigrant from Ireland with very little formal education.

He declined the nomination for a fourth term of Mayor of Indianapolis and as the century entered its last decade, Tom Taggart began to expand his interests to the building of his own health resort in the French Lick/ West Baden valley.

Chapter 13

The French Lick Springs Hotel Company

In April 1900, Tom Taggart and three partners, W.M. McDoel, president of the Monon Railroad, Crawford Fairbanks, owner of a brewery in Terre Haute, and Colonel L.T. Dickason, owner and operator of rock quarries in Indiana and Illinois, purchased an 80 acre tract of land near the French Lick Hotel property that was owned by the Louisville syndicate. Some accounts say that Tom Taggart had offered to buy the French Lick Hotel property but when the owners declined his offer, that is when he started planning to build a third hotel in the Baden/Lick valley. This account hints that because the French Lick Springs Company did not feel they could compete with a third hotel, they gave in and sold the property to Tom Taggart and his three associates. Whatever the incentive, Tom Taggart and the French Lick Springs Hotel Company did buy the hotel at French Lick in 1901 and immediately started an expansion program that turned the previous hotel around…literally. The original hotel had faced the springs on the north, but in 1901, with the expansion of the east side of the hotel the entrance to the hotel was moved to the side facing east, just as it does today.

The east portion of the Windsor became the front of the hotel and was faced in yellow French Lick Brick. A local historian told me that this brick wasn't actually fired in French Lick but in the Jasper/Huntingburg area.

Wherever the source, that brick was narrower than typical brick, making it more expensive to make and requiring more bricks per square foot. When I returned to French Lick in 2000 and started my 'history sleuthing', I was impressed when I saw that even the power plant had been faced in this more expensive brick.

Mud, Flood, and Sabotage

Where Mother Nature had been the cause of a severe drought in 1897, wreaking havoc on the flow of the Pluto Spring, she turned around to dump torrential rains on Tom Taggart's hotel in 1902, flooding the entire valley and causing extensive damage to the hotel. Tom Taggart, in boots and rain gear joined many of his workers in trying to protect the hotel property.

In the summer of 1903 the water at the springs again began to diminish but not due to a drought. The syndicate from Louisville, after selling the property had a change of heart and wanted to re-purchase the hotel. That was NOT going to happen.

One of the previous owner stated, "…I will sink old Pluto to hell.", and that is what they set out to do. To achieve that end, they drilled wells on property next to the hotel's property, intercepting the flow of mineral water that fed the springs at the French Lick Springs Hotel and then pumping the mineral water into the French Lick Creek, thus cutting off the flow of mineral water to Pluto, Proserpine, and Bowles springs. The mineral water was being wastefully dumped at the rate of over half a million gallons a day. Taggart with The French Lick Springs Hotel Company brought an injunction against these men, took them to court and was granted a perpetual injunction.

While I was telling this to a group of people on the history tour, an attorney in the group said that he was familiar with this court case and it is still used today as a precedent for cases against wasting of natural resources.

Pluto and the Red Devil

As the mineral water again returned to its previous rate of flow, Tom Taggart could now concentrate his efforts on improving the hotel. A new power house was built, new furnishings for the hotel were purchased, and the sale of Pluto water using the name "PLUTO" and the picture of a red devil representing the god Pluto were registered trademarks.

In 1903 improvements were made to the bottling plant and Pluto Water was being bottled there in concentrated form for sale all over the United States. This plant was in use until the bottling plant that is across the street from the hotel was built in 1913. The extravagant claims of the past for Pluto water were becoming more realistic, being now tooted, oops, *touted* as the WORLD'S GREATEST LAXATIVE.

Guests would often stay at the resort for two weeks or more in order to fully enjoy the benefits of drinking the Pluto water and taking the Pluto baths.

Sole Ownership

Mr. Taggart's interest in the hotel was very personal but his partners were wealthy men who saw the hotel simply as an investment. When Taggart wanted to continue expanding the hotel his partners disagreed, wanting to use profits to pay dividends on their investments. When he offered to buy them out, they wanted five times their initial investment and they wanted it in 10 days. Tom Taggart set about borrowing from various sources and came up with the amount in time to buy the hotel. Taggart was able to pay off all of the loans in just three years from the hotel profits.

By 1905 the French Lick Springs Hotel was completely in his control and he could move forward with more additions to the property. That year a six-story annex was added to the south end of the front of the hotel and a sixth floor was added to the entire front wing. The bath house and power house were expanded and Pluto, Proserpine, and Bowles spring houses were rebuilt.

Along with promoting Pluto Water, Taggart wanted the resort to start expanding its appeal to include the other benefits that the resort had to offer. Guests were encouraged to relax on the wide front porch and to enjoy the beautiful gardens in a stress-free atmosphere. The more active folks could participate in a game of tennis, go horseback riding, or play a round of golf.

Golf in the USA.

At the beginning of the 20th century, golf in the United States was just starting to gain popularity. The first 18-hole course was built in Wheaton, Illinois at The Chicago Golf Club in 1893. Three years later, when Taggart bought the French Lick Springs Hotel there was a nine-hole golf course only 150 yards from the hotel.

Taggart wanted to promote golf at his hotel so in 1910, Tom Taggart hired Scottish-American, Thomas Bendelow, to turn the nine-hole course into an 18-hole course. Bendelow was a prolific golf course architect in his day, designing 600 courses over the first 35 years of the twentieth century.

As the popularity of golf continued to grow, Tom Taggart added another 18-hole golf course just two miles from the hotel. In 1920, Taggart hired Scottish-American, Donald Ross to design a more challenging course. According to many guests who have played the Donald Ross Course, it is truly challenging. Once I even had a hot, tired, frustrated golfer approach my desk and declare, "That (Donald Ross) course is ALL UPHILL!"

A Master Gardener

When Mr. Taggart was looking for someone to be in charge of his gardens, he tried a number of horticulturists from the Indianapolis area but they didn't have the expertise that Mr. Taggart wanted. Then he discovered Charlie Springer of French Lick. Charlie proved to be a master at growing whatever needed growing. Flowers bloomed in abundance in the Formal Gardens and the Japanese Gardens. Potted plants were placed on the steps leading up to the lobby and plants and cut flowers there seen throughout the hotel. Even the cows could enjoy the beauty of flowers and shrubs that surround the dairy barn.

Mr. Springer was also in charge of the greenhouse that was next to the Pluto Bottling Plant and was a favorite place of mine, especially in the winter. Walking into the warm, humid air, smelling the flowers and seeing the huge rubber tree plant that stood near the front entrance, I felt I had just discovered a tropical island.

The hotel's greenhouse benefited the entire valley providing us with fresh flowers for every occasion. My own wedding flowers, white gardenias, came from the hotel's greenhouse as did every corsage I wore until I moved away from French Lick.

The hotel grew most of their own vegetables and had their own dairy. Buttermilk, which was the milk that was separated from the cream when butter was produced at the hotel's dairy, was offered as a beverage at meals. There was also a station near the ninth hole of the golf course where ice cold buttermilk was available for the golfers; a refreshing drink on a hot day.

You can thank the French Lick Springs Hotel for another drink besides Pluto water: Tomato Juice. Prior to 1917, tomato juice was not served in public places; however, I suspect some housewives had been serving it to their families for years. As the story goes, it seems that the hotel had run out of oranges one morning and Chef Louis Perrin, in order to provide fresh juice to his guests, started squeezing tomatoes. Tomato juice soon became so popular as a morning beverage that Chef Perrin began canning the juice in the hotel's kitchen. When Chef Perrin couldn't keep enough jars of juice on the shelf the hotel began 'outsourcing' to Paoli's Tomato Products Company. By the early 1920's another tomato juice canning factory opened in French Lick to help meet the growing demand for tomato juice at the hotel. As the 1920's drew to a close, tomato juice was beginning to be canned commercially by other factories.

My mother didn't talk much about her childhood but one day as she and I were walking downtown we passed a house that was directly across from the post office and Mother said, "I use to take violin lessons from Mrs. Perrin in that house."

I was so surprised that Mother knew how to play the violin; she had never admitted to having any musical training before. It wasn't until I had returned to French Lick and was researching the hotel's history that I again ran across the name Perrin. While doing the trolley tour, one of the drivers pointed out Chef Perrin's house and at that moment I realized that she had taken violin lessons from his wife.

I knew that Mother's family had not had much money beyond the necessities, and I remember wondering now the family had been able to afford a violin. That answer came recently when I was reminded that my great-grandfather, Ulysses Morton Bell, had played the violin and must have given my mother one of his. Grandpa Bell was the only grandparent I ever knew and I always felt a sense of awe when I was around him.

The Hotel and the Town

The relationship between the hotel and town has always been close. Without the hotel there may have never been a town at all. There really wasn't much to attract people to this smelly, wet valley except to hunt for game. For a while, the state envisioned yielding salt from the spring water, but despite every method used to extract salt from the water, the yield just wasn't worth the effort.

Then along came Doctor Bowles and in the middle of a mineral water swamp there arose a harbinger to the magnificent resort that people are still coming to nearly two centuries later.

Doctor Bowles was responsible for the surveying of his land and platting the town of French Lick in March 1857. Whatever footprints on history

Doctor Bowles may have left, his foresight and promotion of the springs at French Lick are why we have the French Lick Springs Resort and the town of French Lick today.

The period of time between Bowles and Taggart, 1857 to 1900, doesn't report much about the tie between the town and hotel. But in 1901 Tom Taggart quickly picked up the mantle and continued the close bond between hotel and town.

The first thing he did was offer to sell electricity to the town. The hotel's new power plant was capable of generating enough electricity for both the hotel and town. Taggart put up the poles and wires, free of charge, and provided all maintenance for the utility, free of charge, for a period of 25 years.

The hotel built an electric streetcar line between French Lick and West Baden, providing a link between the two towns, giving transportation for locals and hotel guests of both towns. The fare was a nickel.

Then in 1905, Mr. Taggart offered to lay pipes and fire hydrants and supply water to the town, connecting the town to the hotel's water supply. As the hotel continued to improve so did the town.

In 1910-1911, another addition was built onto the six-story annex that housed the ladies' bath on the first floor and the men's bath and pool were on the floor below. Today, the spa is where the ladies' bath had been and the bowling alley and recreation center are where the men's bath had been. The men's pool once occupied the room where the present work-out room is located. One can still see the stained glass in the spa and rec room bar that enhanced the former bath areas.

Tom Taggart's interests had extended beyond the hotel proper to include developing more highway systems. He and Carl G. Fisher were among the delegates appointed to the Dixie Highway Association that was striving to develop the Dixie Highway from Detroit to Homestead, Florida. Taggart had even hoped to build what is now the Indianapolis Speedway in the

French Lick valley but the hills didn't provide any flat place large enough for the track.

During the 1910-1911 expansion, the north side of the wrap-around front porch was enclosed and an addition was built to replace the wood frame wing facing the springs. Another feature of this new wing was an entrance from the gardens that gave access to the new "Pluto Bar". Pluto water was piped directly from the spring to this room so guest could enjoy the water without going outside in severe weather. The ceiling to the area where the Pluto Bar stood was shaped like the inside of a Pullman car because guests had most likely arrived via the train.

Trains and Planes

I could always tell when it was time for the Kentucky Derby by the large number of train cars that would be on the parking tracks near the hotel. Some guests even had their own private train cars for their trip to watch the "Run for the Roses".

With French Lick being only 50 miles from Churchill Downs, many guests came to stay at the French Lick Springs Hotel before going to the Kentucky Derby. There would be train cars available to take the guests in comfort to the Derby, allowing them to just enjoy the ride and not having to fight the crowds in Louisville.

If it had not been for the accessibility of train travel it is very doubtful that French Lick could have survived. At one time there were fourteen trains arriving daily in French Lick, three of these trains traveled round trip from Chicago alone. Among the names of celebrities who visited the hotel were Joseph and Rose Kennedy, Walter Hagen, and Irving Berlin.

There was also a small airport where private air planes could land. Two famous guests who arrived by plane were Howard Hughes and his passenger, Lana Turner, minus luggage. He was flying a civilian version of the P-12B pursuit aircraft. Of course the entire population of the valley was excited over any airplane that arrived but especially when such well-known passengers were onboard. After a brief stay at the hotel, they prepared to fly out of French Lick. As Hughes walked past a group of local men one of them said in an aside to his friends, "He'll never git that thing off the ground." referring to the shortness of runway. Hughes must have overheard the remark because as he began to take off he revved up the motor, sped down the runway, and at the last moment lifted off…proving he could "git that thing off the ground".

Not everyone coming to the springs stayed in the French Lick Springs Hotel or West Baden Springs Hotel. Many people visiting the springs were of a lesser social and financial status than the Joe Kennedys, the Irving Berlins and Howard Hughes. This influx of people gave the local residents the opportunity to benefit financially by providing more affordable housing for these visitors to the valley. Brochures listed the names of 18 additional hotels and boarding houses; 8 in West Baden, 2 of which were for "colored people"; and 10 alterative places to stay in at French Lick.

According to the brochures, the West Baden Springs Hotel rates started at $3.00 per day and the capacity was 1,200 guests. French Lick Springs Hotel's rates started at $4.00 per day and they could accommodate between 600 and 700 guests. The remaining 18 hotels and boarding houses advertised room rates starting at $1.00 per day upwards. The total capacity in both major hotels and the 18 smaller hotels and boarding houses numbered over 3,330 guests; and that did not count the three hotels that listed no numbers for the capacity of their hotels. The guests to the valley could well outnumber the combined population of these two small towns.

Senator Taggart

Tom Sr.'s vision for the resort was a place for rest, relaxation, and recreation. This was a place away from the concerns of business, a chance to recharge one's mind and body. Where some people might enjoy a good round of golf or attending a baseball game, Tom Taggart's favorite form of recreation was politics.

In 1916, Tom Taggart was appointed United States Senator to fill the unexpired term of Benjamin F. Shively. Shively had died with less than a year remaining in his term, so Mr. Taggart, the former *Mayor* Tom Taggart now was *Senator* Tom Taggart.

While in high School I was honored to be one of the students to attend Hoosier Girls' State. I ran for the state senate and won. When I went to the opening session of the senate, I was told that I was a "freshman" senator and would not be allowed to speak. I was surprised, and silently piqued, that being a "freshman" senator prohibited me from full participation in the work of the senate.

Tom Taggart must have had similar feelings during the short time that he was a United States Senator. However, Tom Taggart ignored the unwritten-time-honored code of conduct and let his voice be heard, much to the chagrin of the more "senior" senators. Some were so offended by his speaking out in reference to wasteful government spending that they actually got up and walked out in protest.

Taggart ran for the next term but was defeated by the Republican candidate. He also ran again in 1920 but was again defeated.

Surviving Prohibition

With the enactment of the national constitutional ban on the production, importation and sale of alcoholic beverages that began in 1920, many hotels were struggling to keep solvent. The French Lick Springs Hotel however, continued to profit with more than 100,000 guests visiting the French Lick Springs Hotel annually in the 1920's. One reason the impact of prohibition didn't reach the French Lick Springs Hotel was that Tom Taggart had never allowed alcohol to be served at his hotel. Taggart wasn't a moralist; alcohol just wasn't compatible with the healthy discipline people came to the hotel to enjoy.

The drink that may have kept the French Lick Springs Hotel alive during this time was actually Pluto Water. Over 450 car loads of Pluto water were shipped by rail in 1919 and sales continued to increase during the following years. The little green bottle with the picture of the French Lick Springs Hotel and the "Red Devil" on the label was putting advertisement in nearly every drug store in the country. The name of the French Lick Springs Hotel was recognized throughout the United States.

The Taggarts At The Port

Beginning in the early years of the 20th century, the Taggart family would spend most of the summer months on Cape Cod, first leasing a house in the village and later, in 1912, buying property where the Port View Hotel had once stood. The estate was built on the point and has a wonderful view of the harbor and ocean. Tom named the main house, Amyvale, after the village where he was born in Ireland. As the family grew, a cottage on the compound was named Overflow Cottage and was given to their daughter, Nora Taggart Chambers and her growing family.

In 1928 the Taggarts got new next-door neighbors at the Port, Joe and Rose Kennedy. Mr. and Mr. Kennedy had been guests at the French Lick Springs Hotel in 1925. Joe Kennedy and Tom Taggart had a lot in common: both men were of Irish decent, both Democrats, and both strong leaders in the Democratic Party. But their ideas of what was best for the Party often collided as they were looking out for different geographical locations. Their religions may have also been a factor as they looked 'for the greater good', Kennedy – Catholic, and Taggart – Protestant. Kennedy even joined forces with William Randolph Hurst against Taggart.

It wasn't long after the death of Tom, Sr. that Joe Kennedy entered into a controversy with the Taggart family over a right-of-way on his property. It was settled out of court but didn't do much to improve the Taggart-Kennedy relationship. There was some interaction between the Taggart children and the Kennedy children, visiting back and forth between the two complexes, even some dating but very little in the way of close friendships.

Chapter 14

The Generosity Of Tom Taggart

Tom Taggart had a remarkable gift for remembering peoples' names. That gift was not only helpful in the field of politics but also in his relationship with his employees. He would often be seen walking throughout the hotel and grounds, stopping to talk with an employee and asking about their family. There are many stories about Taggart helping alleviate financial hardships and even paying for surgeries for those in need. When Tom Taggart owned the hotel no employee ever lost his or her job due to illness or mandatory retirement.

There are many stories about the generosity of Tom Taggart and one of them hits very close to home, literally. When my father was a young man with four small children, ages 6, 4, 2, and a new born infant, he won a motorcycle. One day while riding to work, as he rounded a turn on the street below the Catholic Church he was hit by a car. The bike fell over, pinning his ankle under the motorcycle. The local doctor's office was just a block away from the scene of the accident and someone ran to him, asking him to come to Daddy's aid. This was 1920, long before any form of a "rescue squad" or EMT would be on the scene. The doctor rushed to him, and seeing the condition of the ankle warned him not to step on that foot but Daddy being Daddy tried to stand. When my father told me this story he said, "The bones in my ankle were crushed and when I stood they all just crumbled." Daddy was sent to Indianapolis and was hospitalized for a month.

After returning home his ankle was still in a cast and Daddy couldn't walk except with the aid of crutches. It was during that time when early one cold morning in April, the flu caught on fire at my father's home. It was all that the family could do to get out with just the clothes on their backs. Daddy said the firemen couldn't save the house, but they kept spraying water on a trunk that held the baby's clothes. That trunk was the only thing saved. He would laugh as he recalled that baby clothes were about the only thing well-meaning neighbors gave them following the fire.

Tom Taggart wanted Daddy to bring his family to live in the hotel while they were without a home but Daddy wouldn't hear of it; he would have felt very out of place living at the hotel. So Mr. Taggart bought a house and then offered to sell the house to Daddy and he could pay some from each paycheck until it was paid for. That house is the house where my father reared his first family and it was also the home where Tommie and I grew up.

A Legacy

When Tom Taggart, Sr. passed away on March 6, 1929, he left what was a substantial sum of money for that time to several of his employees including my father. With the money my father inherited he built four adjoining garages behind our home.

The Playhouse

Daddy turned one of the garages into a playhouse and it was a magical place for a little child.

Our home, like most homes in French Lick and West Baden, was built on the side of a hill. Daddy built wooden stairs with a banister leading up from the backyard to the little front porch outside of the front door of the playhouse. A beautiful lilac tree reached all the way up to the front porch and when in bloom the lilacs were at eye and nose level so I could enjoy the lovely fragrance as I sat on my little porch. I think I enjoyed the porch as much as I enjoyed the inside of the playhouse. I felt like I was sitting in a tree house.

The playhouse had a double wood floor and two rooms. The front room had a wood-burning stove. There was a small wooden couch, doll beds, and a chair and dresser, all of them Daddy had built in his basement workshop in the pre-dawn hours of winter. The second room had a full-sized pump organ and my old, metal crib where I put various dolls, (let them suffer in that hard, cold, metal bed and see how they like it.)

That crib was the most hateful object of my childhood. I was in that darn crib for my first five years of life. I slept in a bedroom that I shared with my parents because Aunt Betty had the other bedroom. My crib was made out of metal, cold and hard, that startled me awake whenever a wayward foot or hand would slip out from under the covers and touch that cold, hard, metal crib. To add mental anguish to metal anguish, when I was three years old my mother's brother, Edward Morton, died at age 23 while living somewhere in northern Indiana. It was the custom back then to bring the loved one home for the viewing and funeral so Uncle Mort was put on display in our home. I remember my father holding me up in his arms so I could see Uncle Mort's body in the casket. That is a sight every three-year-old really needs to see. This was the first and only time I remember meeting Uncle Mort. In my little three-year-old mind I thought the casket looked like my crib and I thought it was sitting where my crib sat. I have finally come to the conclusion that it was probably in the living room, not in the corner of the bedroom that I shared with my parents, because that just doesn't make sense, but I *thought* it was my crib because it was just like my crib, cold and hard. That is when I started worrying that my parents would die and leave me alone. One day I told my mother, "I hope I die before you and Daddy." but she said that would make them so very sad and I shouldn't wish such a thing. After that I kept my wish a secret.

The one good thing that came from the passing of Uncle Mort was Punky, his chow-chow dog. Punky was Uncle Mort's puppy and when he passed we inherited that little red ball of fur. When Punky lost Uncle Mort, he adopted my father as his master. Chows are usually one-owner dogs and Punky was no exception. He did tolerate me and even let me dress him up a tad. But overall he was a no nonsense dog, regal and loyal.

The summer before I learned to read, I was sitting in my playhouse looking at a magazine. The cover showed people enjoying a summer day and having some kind of celebration. I had to ask my mother what a word on the cover said and she told me, "June." I don't know what caused me to do what came next, but, I decided the people on the magazine cover were having a JUNE PARTY and somehow I knew that month was coming up, so I blissfully went around the neighborhood, inviting folks to my "June Party" on June 1st. Fortunately, one of the neighbors called my mother and asked if she could bring anything to the party. It had never occurred to me that I needed to tell my parents about the party, they never consulted me when they had a party. When my mother told my father what I had done, he said, "Okay, I guess we are having a party." We had quite an assortment of guests that day, from a family with a new born baby all the way up to "Grandma" Pruitt, who lived across the street and was 90 years old. My father and some other men had to carry Grandma Pruitt up the hill to our house. We had hot dogs cooked on the outdoor grill that my father had constructed in our backyard and bottles of pop cooled in the big washtub filled with ice. Dessert was roasted marshmallows. There may have been other food served but I only cared about the burned hot dogs, burned marshmallows and orange pop. After the party I was strongly advised to consult with my parents BEFORE I invited guests in the future.

chapter 15

Thomas Douglas Taggart

The only son of Tom and Eva Taggart was born July 16, 1886, the fifth child of their six children. He attended public school in Indianapolis, Howe Military School in Indiana and Betts Academy in Connecticut, going on to attend Yale where he graduated with a Ph.B from the university's Sheffield Scientific School.

Tom Sr.'s lack of advantages when growing up could have been a handicap, but Tom, Sr. had turned every lack into an asset. He and his wife were concerned that their son had had too many advantages so when Tom, Jr. joined his father at the hotel in 1909, he started working in the storeroom; his father wanted him to learn the hotel business from the bottom to the top.

Thomas D. learned his lessons well and began taking on more and more of the responsibilities of running the hotel; overseeing the 1910-1911 expansion of the west wing that faced the springs.

Although the younger Tom Taggart was much less outgoing than his father, he still had the most important quality that had made the hotel a success, he cared.

Tom Sr. and Tom Jr. not only cared for the enjoyment of the hotel's guests, they cared about the people who worked for them. They knew that the attitude of hospitality started from the top. Even the workers who might never see a guest *did* see the Taggarts walking among them, working among them, engaging in conversation, asking about their families. The Taggarts showed respect and concern for their employees and in turn, the employees had respect and concern for the Taggarts. You see, respect is a two-way street.

My mother told me that Mr. Taggart came to our house to see me soon after I was born. She said he remarked on the red in my hair. I use to think about his noticing that I had red tones in my hair, putting my thought-emphasis on that, until I came to realize how special it was to have Tom Taggart, Jr. come to our home to see Frank McDonald's new baby girl.

Tom and his wife, Adele, were married in June 8, 1922, and they became parents of daughter, Eva, on August 5, 1923, the birthday of her grandmother, Mrs. Eva Taggart.

1929 a Year of Mourning

Thomas D. suffered two devastating loses in 1929; the loss of his father and the loss of his wife. His father passed away on March 6, 1929, leaving Tom with the full responsibility of the hotel. Then on July 5, 1929, Adele took her own life leaving Tom with the full responsibility of his daughter who turned 6 years old one month after her mother's death. His sister, Lucy, who never married, along with governesses, helped in the care of his daughter, Eva.

In September of 1929, Tom moved from the apartment in the hotel into the new home that his father had built for him atop of the hill where a 100 foot observation tower had stood. This hilltop is the second highest elevation in Indiana and was a popular scenic picnic area at one time. The tower was torn down and the lumber was used in the building of the thoroughbred horse barn. The home was named Mt. Airie and was built in the style of the Taggart's summer home in Hyannis Port. I have heard that there are secret passages that would allow Thomas D. to escape from his home if threatened by someone, such as members of organized crime.

Today the home is the center of the Pete Dye Golf Course.

Not So "Happy Days"

Just as the song, "Happy Days Are Here Again" was being published; the foundation of postwar prosperity was becoming as shaky as the shimmy and other dance steps of the popular Charleston. Excess and avoidance of what would prove to be portents of a coming crash were being ignored. "Black Thursday", October 24, 1929 was the beginning of the end of the roaring twenties that let out its final roar on October 29, 1929, also known as "Black Tuesday", with the collapse of the New York Stock Exchange.

The French Lick Springs Hotel's broker's office located just off of the hotel's lobby was kept busy trying to keep informed as to what was happening in New York. Needless to say, it was close to mayhem at both the French Lick and West Baden hotels. Soon guests began leaving to return to their homes. Porters were kept busy carrying luggage to awaiting automobiles and to the train depot. Contrary to some newspaper headlines, no one in either hotel "jumped" to their death. Women cried and men swore but no one committed suicide. However, the "crash" did cripple business at many hotels, especially at West Baden.

Charles "Ed" Ballard had bought the West Baden Springs Hotel in 1922. The exodus that began on Black Thursday never turned around for Ballard and as the days following the crash began to turn into weeks and months, West Baden's hotel continued to be practically empty. By 1932, Ballard was ready to sell the hotel but there were no buyers, so he "sold" the hotel to the Society of Jesus for $1.00 and the hotel became West Baden College, a seminary for Jesuit priests.

At French Lick the second Tom Taggart was determined to keep providing a place for people to visit and enjoy AND a place for the people of the valley to continue to be employed. Instead of pinching pennies, Tom Taggart started spending those pennies in advertising.

On June 1, 1931, French Lick hosted the annual Democratic Governors' Conference that included the governor from New York, Franklin Delano Roosevelt. It was probably at this conference where F.D.R. received the nod from the other governors to run for the office of President of the United States. This conference received national coverage in newspapers and in every movie theatre via the Movietone Newsreel that was covering the event.

Movietone Newsreel also covered the pre-Kentucky Derby activities in the 1930's which, again, gave the French Lick Springs Hotel national advertisement.

The request for convention services had been increasing since the early 1920's, so Thomas D. Taggart was put in charge of what would be the last addition of the Taggart era. In 1924 this new addition was on the north side of the main wing and had a large convention hall equipped with a stage, four floors for guest rooms, and space for parlors for small meetings. The foresight of building the convention hall wing was paying off as political and business conventions were coming to French Lick.

Tom Jr. began putting more emphasis on golf as P.G.A. and Mid-West Amateur Golf Championships were coming to French Lick. Tom also added a skeet club to the already existing activities of tennis and horseback riding.

The vacationing public no longer wanted a two-week stay of rest and relaxation but more of a change of pace from the usual hubbub of day-to-day existence. Tom, Jr. had to meet the challenge of the new requirements of vacationers and convention attendees, and at the same time preserve the tradition of healthful surroundings. Mineral water continued to be part of the appeal of French Lick, just not the main one.

"Take Me Out To The Ballgame"

With the onset of World War II, many minor league baseball teams stopped playing altogether but President Roosevelt considered the "national pastime" a help with homeland moral and encouraged major league baseball to continue. As it turned out, major league baseball was also a great moral booster to our military. These young men would follow their teams and for brief moments share something about "home".

Even though major league players were exempt from the draft, 500 major league players and 2,000 minor league players served in the military.

Teams were required to travel to spring training and games by cars, leaving trains for the transportation of troops and supplies. Gasoline was rationed so travel became limited by the baseball commissioner, Kennesaw M. Landis, and the director of the federal Office of Defense Transportation, Joseph B. Eastman, to keep teams close to their home bases. The Cardinals, White Sox and Cubs had to stay in Missouri, Indiana, and Illinois. The Cubs and White Sox chose to come to French Lick for their spring training in 1943-1944. In 1945 the Sox moved their spring training to Terra Haute and the Cubs returned to French Lick. Weather was wet and cold with Lost River often filling its dry beds to overflowing. There were even times when practice had to be held in the convention hall.

While the Cubs were in French Lick, they were treated to the Pluto bathes, and remember, they did win the pennant in 1945.

I'm just say'n….it couldn't hurt.

chapter 16

Gambling In French Lick? I Am Shocked!

In addition to mineral water, golf, skeet shooting, baseball, conventions and the many advertised activities that brought people to the resort, there was another enticement that drew people to the French Lick/West Baden valley, but it wasn't advertised. In fact, a lot of people didn't even know it existed. Well, maybe not *a lot* of people; maybe only one or two. I was one of those people and the other person was the Chief of Police.

Things at my home were pretty much on a need-to-know-basis and there was much that my parents felt that I did not need to know. If I spoke out of turn, which meant entering into the adult conversation without being invited, I was told, "Children are to be seen and not heard." If I walked into a conversation where the subject was something the adults thought I shouldn't hear, someone would say, "Little pitchers have big ears" and the conversation would stop. I didn't know that the handle on a pitcher was sometimes called an ear, so I thought they were saying that **I** had big ears and that hurt my feelings.

There were times that I had questions but my mother was an expert at circumventing answers that might require more explaining.

The family that lived on the hill behind our house intrigued me. I was not allowed to go visit them; I even knew enough not to invite them to my June party. They had a very nice, big house, bigger that anyone else in the neighborhood. From my back yard I had seen their children who were a lot older than me, more the age of my Aunt Betty who lived with us, but I had never seen them go to school with Aunt Betty. One day I got curious and I asked Mother where they went to school? She said, "I think they go to school in Indianapolis." So that started me thinking some more and I figured that with that big house and kids who went to school in Indianapolis, they must be rich. So I asked Mother, "What does Mr. Thacker do for a living?" Mother lowered her voice and said in a whisper, "I think he owns a liquor store." Well, I knew enough about liquor that it was bad and no one was allowed to talk about that. So that kept me from asking any further questions.

As it turned out, Mr. Thacker was managing the Brown Casino that was owned by Ed Ballard. But for the story of gambling in French Lick/West Baden we need to go back a few more years, to 1901.

Tom Taggart, Sr. had inherited a 'casino' or 'club house' when he and his partners bought the hotel. The Pavilion was located between the Pluto and Proserpine Springs, and had been built by the French Lick Springs Company in 1888. On the first floor was a gymnasium, bowling alley and a large glass enclosed dance floor. The casino was on the second floor with a walkway or ramp connecting the front of the hotel to the second floor of the Pavilion.

At the 1904, Democratic Convention, Tom Taggart was elected Chairman of the Democratic Nation Committee. At this same convention William Randolph Hearst was hoping to be the Democratic presidential candidate to run against Republican President Theodore Roosevelt. Taggart, however, did not support Hearst for the presidential post and Hearst got mad. About the only thing worse than a woman scorned is a politician scored....especially if he owns the largest newspaper chain in the United States. In 1906, Hearst used his newspapers to launch a smear campaign against Taggart. His use of yellow press or tabloid journalism included Ed

Ballard and Lee Sinclair's hotel at West Baden Springs. Due to Hearst's claims of gambling at French Lick and West Baden Springs, the Governor of Indiana, Rep. J. Frank Hanley, ordered the two casinos in question to be raided. After which Tom Taggart evicted whoever was leasing the Pavilion and when these accusations were brought to court in July, 1906, both Taggart and Sinclair were exonerated.

I have not found to my satisfaction just who exactly leased or managed this French Lick "casino". There are several differing accounts, but the names, Ed Ballard and Al Brown, keep cropping up. I personally tend toward "Al" Brown.

The reason I lean towards Brown being the one evicted is because following the closing of the casino at French Lick's Pavilion, Brown built the Brown Building, sometimes referred to as Brown Hotel, directly across from the French Lick Hotel's power plant. It was built using yellow brick, not the same as what was used at the French Lick Springs Hotel but similar enough in color to make it look as if it were part of the hotel. This may have been just to aggravate Tom Taggart.

One day while I was at my concierge desk, a gentleman approached me and said he was a descendent of the man who had built the Brown Building. When I asked, "Al Brown?" he said, "He wasn't called 'Al', he went by 'A.H'. Brown." Well that was an interesting bit of news. He said that after A.H. had sold the building to Ed Ballard, he then moved to Louisville, Kentucky and built another hotel in that city.

I have had guests ask me if Al Capone had owned the Brown Building. He diffidently did not. For one thing, the Chicago mob never was able to infiltrate the gaming market in the valley, which was controlled by Charles "Ed" Ballard, but it wasn't for lack of trying. There was one incident where bombs were thrown into the Brown Building and onto the West Baden Hotel Porch but not much damage was done and Ed Ballard was not persuaded to give up control of the gambling in the valley.

My Aunt Lorraine, who was married to my Uncle Alvia, once told me that one day when she was a little girl, some men in a black car drove up to her home. Her father, Cliff Marshall, told her mother to take the children and hide, which they did. The men wanted Cliff to tell them where they could find Ed Ballard. Cliff said that he didn't know where Ed was and the men took Cliff with them to look for Ballard. Aunt Lorraine said she, her mother, brother, and sister were afraid that they would never see their father again. But Cliff was able to convince the men that he really didn't know where Ed Ballard was and the men brought Cliff back home, unscathed.

I found in an old newspaper from 1943 that Cliff Marshall was the manager of the Elite Café, a gaming house owned by one of the Ballads. You might find it of interest to learn that the Chief of Police, William Marshall, was the father of Cliff Marshall.

The Police Station was right across the street from the Brown Building and just a block from the Elite Club where the American Legion is today. When Johnny and I moved back to French Lick in 2000 and we renewed acquaintances with several of my former classmates, I learned just how ignorant I had been on the subject of casinos operating in French Lick and West Baden. I was under the impression that, yes, there had at one time been casinos in the valley but they had all closed when gambling became illegal in Indiana. Now I was learning that gambling had ALWAYS been illegal in Indiana. Some of my school friends' parents had been closely involved in gaming during the 1940's but I didn't have a clue. One time I heard my father mention a 'one-arm bandit', referring to a slot machine, and I thought he was talking about our town's policeman who had only one arm.

Besides the Brown and the Elite Club, the old, dusty filing cabinets that were far back in one corner of a basement room in the hotel started yielding the names of more casinos that were in French Lick and West Baden Springs. There were the Chateau, the Colonial and the Homestead in West Baden, and the Gorge in rural French Lick. The Babylon, blacks only, in French Lick, plus there were many smaller, unnamed backstreet places. Raids had occurred from time to time at various casinos in the valley but this only caused a short respite from the gaming that was going on.

Governor Schricker had promised in his second, nonconsecutive run for Governor, that, if elected, he would end the gambling in Orange County. He was elected. Governor Schricker intended to keep his campaign promise so on the night before the Kentucky Derby in 1949, the Brown Casino was raided, thus closing the most attractive and profitable casino in Orange County. But not all casinos were closed.

According to the June 15, 1950, issue of the *Springs Valley Herald,* the Gorge Inn and the Chateau Club were raided by the Indiana State Police on the night of June 12, 1950, 13 months after the previous raid. Equipment was confiscated and later destroyed. The operators of the games and several other people at each place were taken into custody that night. This may have been the final blow to gambling casinos in the valley for the next 50 years.

As gambling in Indiana was winding down, it was revving up in Las Vegas. From the first hotel-casino, the El Rancho, built in 1941 by Tommy Hull, to Bugsy Siegel's Flamingo, built in 1946, along with the many hotel-casinos that were built with mobsters' money through the 1960's, Las Vegas blossomed in the desert.

I think it is kind of pathetic that I actually had to research the names of casinos in French Lick and West Baden when I had been seeing these buildings all my life but not knowing what they were. I remember sitting in our car with my mother, waiting for my father to come out of the plant and seeing ladies dressed in evening gowns and fur coats, and men wearing tuxedos going to the Brown Building. Mother said they were going to dinner, maybe they were.

Chapter 17

Through The Lens Of
A Movie Camera

I knew very little about the culture that was hiding from me in plain sight but I knew a lot about the world beyond the hills that surrounded French Lick. The world came to me via movies and newsreels at the Dream Theater.

At the Saturday matinee I saw that the west had cowboys, Indians, guns, bows and arrows, and everything was black and white. Like most kids who grew up in the post WWII years, cowboys were our first heroes. Mine were Roy Rogers and Gene Autry. I wanted to *be* either Roy or Gene. Cowgirls didn't interest me much because they didn't get to ride really fast horses. The only time they rode a fast horse was if the horse ran away and a cowboy had to save them, real sissies. And they never got to go on a cattle drive or shoot bad guys. Every Saturday I went to the western matinee, and like the other kids, I would dress appropriately in whatever western garb that I had at my disposal. I wore a western-style shirt, blue jeans or cowgirl skirt (yuck), my cap pistols strapped to my waist, and spurs strapped to my penny loafers. Have you any idea how embarrassing it was to not have cowboy boots for my spurs?

We also had our Super-Heroes, mine was Captain Marvel. One day I had on my Captain Marvel cape (bath towel) and was drinking a glass of cool-aid when I felt super-powers surging through my body. To test my powers, I took a bite out of the glass. When I ran to tell Mother how strong I was, Mother became hysterical. I was as pleased as punch with myself. Did I cut my mouth? Certainly not. I **was** CAPTAIN MARVEL.

On Sunday, I put away my spurs and cap guns and entered the world of color and music with singing and dancing and love. I saw all of the great Broadway musicals and my matinee idols became Mario Lanza and Yul Brenner.

Throughout the week I saw gangster, science fiction, comedy and drama. It was at the movies that I learned about the Ku Klux Klan; how they were responsible for lynching black men and how they burned crosses in the front yards of black sympathizers. I could always identify them because they wore white robes with crosses and white hoods to hide their faces. I had seen it all in movies about the deep south. I was so glad that I lived in the north.

At our theatre, there were a few rows in the back and to the left as you walked down the aisle toward the movie screen where the "colored" people, as we politely called them, always sat.

I often went to the movies by myself or with one other friend but there was one time when I was part of a larger group of girls. I don't remember the occasion but among our group was the one and only black girl in our school. We happily bought our popcorn and giggled our way down the aisle to the center, right, and filed into the row. We had just sat down when the owner of the theatre came down to our row, shined his flashlight at the black girl and said, "*She* has to sit in the colored section." We all just looked at each other in shock. In that one sentence I understood. Finally my eyes were opened and I saw in that darkened movie theatre what I hadn't been able to see in the light of day; people were being treated differently because of their skin color.

I don't remember there being any discussion as we all stood up and moved to the 'colored' section. No one giggled that time.

It was a sobering revelation. I had thought that the black people sat together because they wanted to, not because they had to. The irony is that I had been watching movies that depicted the injustice of segregation in the south while sitting in a theater where segregation was dictated.

I was very much shielded from the prejudice that existed in my beloved valley thanks to my parents. They insisted that I show respect to everyone, calling adults "Sir" or "Ma'am", a person's race didn't matter.

My father, who rarely attended church after his first wife died, had expressed to my mother that when the time came, he wanted the pastor of the African Methodist Episcopal Church or AME Church to preach at his funeral. My father died on July 27, 1970 and at his funeral, one of the guests got up and walked out of the service when the black pastor stood up to preach. Obviously, prejudice was still very much alive. Even in the summer of 1975, a series of cross-burnings plagued both West Baden and French Lick.

My mother allowed me to go to a lot of movies, partly as an escape for me. When I was old enough, I could walk to the afternoon matinee and then telephone her from the upper drug store when the movie was over to let her know I was on my way home. Sometimes she would walk me most of the way, stop and watch me until I was ready to turn the corner to go half of a block to the theater. After the movie and the required phone call she would then walk to meet me half way home.

But before I was old enough to go to the movies, I had no escape.

The Family Secret

I suppose most families have secrets that are lurking in some dark closet and my family had ours. At least we thought it was a secret and I suppose it was to some. We certainly never talked about it openly or publicly.

My father, who was very respected by his employer and employees alike, had a demon that controlled our home. He was an alcoholic. Back then not much was known about the disease. It wasn't even thought of as a disease and we would never have used the word "alcoholic" when referring to my father. We would say that Daddy "drank", and mother told me that Daddy had not been "drinking" during their courtship and early marriage so she had no idea of Daddy's "problem", another more genteel term. I sometimes doubt that she would have married him if she had known what life would be like. Mother hated alcohol. Her father had been an alcoholic and this had contributed largely to the family's hardships. Eventually two of her brothers and one sister suffered from alcoholism. The two brothers joined AA and became recovering alcoholics; sadly her sister did not and died from complications associated with alcoholism.

My half-sister, Violet told me that after an evening when my father had been doing some heavy drinking with his brother-in-law, her mother, Cynthia, had been pleading for him to stop. When Daddy continued to drink, Cynthia, who had come to the end of her rope, locked herself in the bathroom and slit her wrists. Daddy came out of his stupor and broke the bathroom door open, saving her life.

After this happened, Daddy changed his life style; joining a church and never drinking alcohol again until after Cynthia passed away years later.

I am not sure when he resumed drinking but according to my mother it wasn't until about three years into their marriage. All I know is that as far back as I can remember, Daddy, on many evenings would come home from work, head to the bathroom where he stashed his bottle of Four Roses whiskey in the linen closet and we would be in for a very bad night.

I was 64 years old when Vi shared Daddy's willingness to quit drinking for his first family. My father had been dead over 30 years but I still felt jealous that he would stay sober for his first family but not for us. I also felt sad for the many, many days and nights that were lost to the horrors of addiction imposed on an innocent family. I couldn't imagine my mother resorting to such an extreme as putting her own life in danger nor would I have wanted her to, but in my young mind the only solution I could come up with was for Mother and me to leave Daddy. One night I remember Mother and me doing just that.

In my memory I can still see a little four year old girl and her mother hiding behind a big evergreen tree. Mother had just spotted Daddy's car coming down the street in front of my half-brother's house where we were trying to go for safety.

Women in those days didn't see a way to survive without their husbands. Mother knew firsthand what poverty looked like and Daddy did provide for us, always turning his paycheck over to my mother who then handled all of our finances. It took me many years to realize that what I saw as weakness in my mother for tolerating Daddy's drinking was actually strength. Isn't it interesting how children sometimes blame the parent who isn't abusing, not the one who is? It took me forty years and a good psychiatrist to sort that part out and put the blame where it belonged.

Daddy never missed a day of work because of drinking but we had hell to pay at home. I vividly remember the summer evenings when it would be so hot and we had all of our windows closed tight trying to keep the neighbors from hearing Daddy's drunken ranting and raving. Mother would let me stay outside as long as possible, hoping that Daddy would pass out. Of course, I would be outside all by myself, hearing the yelling from my father. That was when I would turn to my imaginary friend, Danny. Sometimes my real live friend, Joe, would be playing with me and I would be so embarrassed if he happened to hear Daddy yelling, and would try to steer him as far as possible from the house. Of course, between my father, Frank McDonald and Joe's grandfather, Harry Porter, Joe and I had heard about every cuss word in or out of the book. Mother never once raised her voice to Daddy and she never swore. But she would sing hymns, not around Daddy, but more to herself during the day as she did housework. However, she did use one phrase that expressed her desire TO swear, it was one long word, "hellbitchandammit."

Inviting a girlfriend to come to my house on the spur of the moment was out of the question. I needed to make sure that Daddy knew ahead of time. On the few occasions when I did get to have company, Daddy would curtail his thirst for the evening. Later, boyfriends were in danger of being cursed off our front porch if they happened to drop by at the wrong time; one was even threatened with a shot gun. I don't know who that was because he never climbed our front steps a second time.

My worse memory happened when I was three and a half years old and Aunt Betty was still living in our home. Daddy was drinking and was very angry about something. He had loaded a handgun and was threatening to shot Mother and Aunt Betty. I can still see the light of the setting sun coming from the kitchen side of the house, casting the dining room into shadows of fear. No one was protecting me, Mother and Aunt Betty were trying to protect themselves, so I cowered behind the dining room table, which was taller than I. Mother was pleading with Daddy and was finally able to convince him to put the gun away.

Thank God that night didn't end in disaster but it did change things in our home. From that time on, all ammunition was hidden from Daddy. If he wanted to go hunting he would tell Mother what he needed and leave the house. Mother would get the bullets or cartridges and when Daddy came back home she would give them to him.

There was also a change in the heart of that frightened little girl. I continued to love my father dearly but the fear of my father that I felt that night never completely went away.

Chapter 18

Friends And Animals

My best friend was always my Aunt Betty who was 14 years older than I and 14 years younger than her sister, my mother. After graduating from high school Aunt Betty worked for a couple of years at the French Lick Hotel but then moved to Indianapolis leaving me alone and lonely. I didn't like being the only child in my family; I didn't like getting all of the attention, both good and bad. Children in large families may feel differently but I envied my cousins, Sandy and Jackie Charnes, because they had each other plus three younger brothers and a sister.

Daddy built a merry-go-round and teeter-totter in the back yard. He also put up two swings and a trapeze for me to play on. The swings and trapeze were fun but did you ever try to teeter-totter by yourself? I did. It doesn't work. I tried sitting on one end of the teeter-totter and using my legs to push up, jumping from a sitting position into the highest altitude I could manage and then landing with a sharp "thud", smacking my bottom on the seat of the teeter-totter as it made a hard landing on the ground, jarring my body all the way up to the top of my head. Sometimes you just need a friend.

I think my father was influenced by Tom Taggart Jr.'s daughter, Eva, who had a pet chicken named "Alice", because he put up a pen in our back yard and stocked it with chickens and other feathered creatures. He called it a "menagerie" and it had Henny-penny, Cocky-locky, Turkey-lurkey,

Ducky-lucky, and Goosey-loosey. One day I let myself into the pen when those foul fowls attacked me and started pecking the buttons on my dress and my little polished fingernails and scared me half to death. It was a happy day for me when those feathered fiends were taken to a farm.

Daddy then brought home some box turtles and put them where the menagerie had been. They thrived there and I really enjoyed them. I wasn't afraid of them and to this day, if I see one trying to cross a road I will stop and take him to safety.

Next he brought home a screech-owl in a bird cage and showed us how the owl could turn his head almost completely around.

The funniest thing Daddy brought home was a bat that someone at the plant had captured. Daddy came carrying it into the kitchen in a bird cage and as we were looking at it, the bat got out of the cage. With one foot Daddy kicked open the kitchen door and at the same time kicked the bat out of the door with the other foot, simultaneously, both feet in the air and he didn't even fall. That's when I learned how fast a "bat out of...the kitchen door" could go.

There were occasional visits with cousins, nieces and nephews but my most consistent playmate was Joseph Porter Noel. Joe and I were the same age. He spent his summers with his grandparents, Harry, whom everyone called "Skinny" and Asta, whom everyone called "Esty" Porter, our next-door neighbors.

Joe was an only child like me (this was before my brother was born). His pet name for me was, "Ebb, old squirrel" and I have no idea where that came from. His Grandfather worked at the Pluto Bottling Plant and Joe and his grandfather were great fishing buddies. Every time I think about Joe, I can still see him taking a stance on the up-side of the hill above the weeping willow tree. He then, I don't know why, began running down the hill towards the back of his grandparents' house gaining speed, running faster and faster until "CRASH!" he flew headfirst through the glass window and landed on Esty's dining room table!

At almost the same moment of landing Joey began yelling, "I'm sorry, I'll pay for the window!" Of course, his grandparents were only concerned that he was alright but I was impressed that he immediately wanted to make restitution for the window. After the initial shock I started laughing and nearly wet my pants. Joey and I played and fought and grew up together until he was old enough to go the Culver Summer Camp, leaving me all alone once more.

Finally, a Baby Brother

December, 1946, my father put a cedar Christmas tree in my playhouse. It had blue lights all over it, not at all like the one in our house that always had multi-colored lights. I loved sitting in the dark looking at my very own special Christmas tree, thinking that I was the luckiest little girl in the world. Shirley Goldman, a high school student who was the daughter of friends of our family was visiting us for a few days. When I work up on a snowy Saturday morning four days before Christmas, I discovered that my parents were not at home and Shirley was there to take care of me. My parents had gone to 'get' a baby. When Daddy came home alone he told me that I had a baby brother. I was not thrilled. I had wanted a baby sister but Daddy told me that they only had boys at the hospital when they went there that day. I couldn't understand why they didn't just wait until the hospital had a girl baby. Mother had tried to prepared me that they were going to 'get' a baby and the name they had decided to name the baby, if it was a girl, was Pamela Sue. My brother was named Thomas Franklin. As a consolation, I named my Christmas doll Pamela Sue, but she was a poor substitute for a real live sister. I never developed much of an interest in that doll because I found that a real live brother was a lot more fun to have around. He was much more challenging, too. Many times I would show him off, having him do cheers with me the one and only year I got to be a cheerleader. I tried to teach him to play the piano and to twirl the baton. He refused to continue with the twirling lessons the day he got hit in the head from a toss I was teaching him.

Even though there was almost nine years between our ages I was still so happy to finally not be an "only child". The older we have become the large gap between our ages has shrunk.

The End of an Era

Just three weeks before the birth of my brother, the hotel was sold by Thomas D. Taggart, ending forty-five years of Taggart family ownership. I'm sure this must have been a time of uncertainty for my parents as it would have been for the entire French Lick valley. My father had worked for both Taggarts since he was 17 years old. Who would have imagined that after working at the hotel for 38 years that Frank McDonald would still be going to work at the hotel for the next 22 years.

Between Taggart and the Sheraton

Thomas D. Taggart sold the hotel in November of 1946, to a New York syndicate headed by John Cabot, of the Cabot Shipping Company. Cabot was also associated with hotels in Syracuse and Utica, New York and the Floridian Hotel at Miami Beach, Florida.

In this post-war period, hotels across the United States were finally able to put much needed improvements into their hotels. This new French Lick Hotel Company made the mistake of not doing much to improve the French Lick hotel. They appeared to be more concerned with showing a profit but not putting those profits back into the hotel.

In 1948 the Pluto bottling plant became the Pluto Corporation. The French Lick Hotel's Castle Knoll Farm, which was located several miles east of French Lick, and the Pluto Corporation were then separated from the French Lick Hotel Company. However, they were still owned by John Cabot.

I remember hearing my father mention the name of "Cabot", and my father taking me to a lodge on the property of the Castle Knoll Farm one colorless winter day. I also remember my father going to Florida and staying in the Floridian Hotel that was owned by Mr. Cabot. Daddy brought home a coconut that was still in the outermost shell. That coconut became our doorstop for the front door of our living room for as long as I can remember.

Though not directly associated with the hotel, the Brown Casino had been part of the attraction for hotel guests for many years. However, the raid in 1949 that closed the Brown resulted in fewer guests checking in at the hotel. Profits fell and debts mounted.

In 1950, the French Lick Hotel Company was hit with a foreclosure suit by the Massachusetts company that had loaned money for the purchase of the hotel. The hotel went into receivership and was managed by Mr. Seelbach of Louisville until it was bought by the Sheraton Corporation in late 1954.

Of course, I was totally unaware of all of the upheaval that was going on at the hotel. I remember hearing the name of Mr. Seelbach, but I was spared the details of all the uncertainty my father must have been feeling about his future.

chapter 19

The French Lick
Sheraton Hotel

In late 1954, the hotel was sold to the Sheraton Corporation becoming The French Lick Sheraton Hotel. Sheraton closed the hotel for three months, giving it a "face-lift".

Inside the hotel ceilings were being lowered in the halls to cover the transom windows that were above the doors to the guest rooms, room air conditioners were added throughout the hotel, and stylish furniture was added. The lobby was brought up to the fifties-look with the black and white tile floor and fifties-style light fixtures. Everything from top to bottom was changed to reflect the "modern" look of the fabulous fifties.

In addition to all of the changes being made to the interior of the hotel, a major change was taking place right outside; Sheraton was installing a swimming pool smack dab in front of the hotel.

Prior to this time guests who wanted to swim had to walk through the formal gardens at the back of the hotel and climb a narrow path up a steep hill to what had been the Taggart's private pool. This new location for the pool would be much more convenient and would be one of the first things arriving guests would see, presenting a picture of fun and relaxation.

The only hitch in the plan was that the water table was so high in that area that following a heavy rain during the construction of the pool, the cement pool actually floated up from its bed. This was clearly not a good place for the pool but Sheraton was determined to put it there. Sheraton triumphed, at least for several years, until patching cracks in the pool's bottom got too tedious. That is when Sheraton built another pool with a retractable dome that allowed swimmers to enjoy the pool year round. This dome pool was on the spring side of the hotel and served guests until 2005 when it was demolished during the hotel's restoration.

In the summer of 1957 I was hired as one of the three life guards at the Cabana pool. This was about the closest I had ever been to the hotel proper. My father was very strict when it came to "knowing my place", and my place was not in the hotel.

Earlier that year in April, a young Pete Dye had won the Midwest Amateur Golf Tournament that was held annually on the Donald Ross Golf Course. Just over 50 years later, the beautiful, challenging Pete Dye Course was opened on top of Mount Airie. The first time I saw what Pete Dye had done to the second highest point in Indiana, the land around the Taggart mansion, I thought, "This man is either a genius or a lunatic." Now I have no doubt, Pete Dye is a GENIUS.

In August of 1957, Hoagie Carmichael came to the hotel and a dinner was held in his honor at the Hill Golf Course, now known as the Donald Ross Golf Course. The hotel's banquet manager asked me to sing with a small band of local musicians at the dinner, and requested that I sing "Stardust", which I did. Poor man; how original was that. However, Hoagie had apparently anticipated my performance and had been stealing himself with beverages to the point that by the time I sang I don't think he even knew I was there.

Pool and Prejudice

Guests had a good view of the pool when they arrived and we at the pool had a good view of new arrivals. One day as I was checking a lady guest in at the pool she looked over to the hotel and happened to see a black family arriving. She glared at me and snapped, "When did 'THEY' start coming here?" I was so shocked I just stood there with my mouth open. She then turned in a huff and I didn't see her again.

It had never occurred to me that anyone would expect our hotel to be "for whites only". Little did I know.

No 'Colored' Allowed

Joe Louis, the world heavy-weight boxing champion from 1937 to 1949, came to French Lick on many occasions. He liked to train here, golf on the Hill Course (Donald Ross Course), and he enjoyed fishing in the creek at West Baden. But Joe was not allowed to stay in the French Lick Hotel. He had to stay at the Waddy Hotel, a hotel for blacks, in West Baden.

The "colored" bar in French Lick, the Babylon, is where my father would sometimes frequent. I've been told that he had to do his drinking in the owner's office because as a white man Daddy wasn't allowed in the bar. Personally, I can't imagine my father being "hidden" in the owner's office. I think if Daddy wanted to sit at the bar he would have been welcomed. I believe that is where Joe Louis may have been when my father saw someone trying to pick a fight with Joe, (whoever that was must have been quite inebriated) and Joe just ignoring him. That incident was so comical to Daddy that he had to share the laugh with Mother and me, forgetting that we weren't supposed to know that he went there.

Sometime in the 1950's the color ban was lifted and the hotel at French Lick was welcoming all guests. Unfortunately, prejudice was still alive as the woman at the pool had demonstrated.

In the summer of 1958 I was again employed at the hotel but this time as the Social Hostess.

That year the Sheraton hosted the first French Lick Women's Open and it was an overwhelming success. I was busy working at the hotel so I never got to see the ladies play but I did get to see them as they returned to the hotel each day after playing on the Donald Ross Golf course and I was *shocked* to hear the language used by some of these ladies. Okay, I was young, naïve, and…..I had never played golf.

I would have preferred to be out at the pool like I was the summer before but this job paid more and it was the job that my father wanted me to have. End of story.

The only advice that my father gave me as I started this new job was to watch out for the "boys in the band" because they all had a girlfriend in every town. In retrospect, I think someone should have warned one of the "boys in the band" about a "girl who was the Social Hostess".

As the Social Hostess I was to greet guests and plan activities for the wives of men who were busy during the day with convention activities. I had card parties, fashion shows, and took them on tours of the Jesuit College that was in the former West Baden Springs Hotel. We couldn't see much of the building because the atrium was considered a cloister and men only were allowed to step foot in the atrium, this excluded even the mothers of the seminarians. We women would stand at one of the entrances where we would be allowed to peek in and see a large statue of Christ in the middle of the atrium. We did get to go into the chapel and walk in the gardens.

Another one of my duties was to be the hostess at afternoon tea. Every day at 4 o'clock afternoon tea was served in the lobby. I would visit with the guests, play the piano and sing. A lovely young black woman was dressed in a "mammy" costume and served the dainty sandwiches and tea. Now I heard guests complaining that we were presenting her as a "slave".

That same summer a young, black bellman said, "Good morning Miss McDonald." to me, and a white guest told me I shouldn't let him speak to me like that. There it was, prejudice again rearing its ugly head.

Music, Music, Music

Sheraton years were very busy years. For two summers the hotel held large music festivals: country, classical and jazz. The jazz festivals were above and beyond what this little valley had ever seen. This was the era of the Newport Jazz Festivals and the one held at French Lick was so big that they only had them for two years, the hotel and the town just couldn't handle the thousands of fans that were invading this little valley. Guests were arriving in droves, many having nowhere to stay. Pullman cars were used for housing, towns' people were renting out rooms, and some guests were camping in tents on the hotel grounds. Everyone who was anyone in the jazz field performed here, including: Dizzy Gillespie, Lionel Hampton, Duke Ellington, and Dave Brubaker. French Lick had never seen anything like it. And we had never seen a "hippie", young men with long hair and beards, sun glasses and sandals. Mercy.

Of course the hotel also had its own band that played in the dining room every night for dinner and later in the lobby for dancing. The tradition of having a hotel band had been around since the 1880's. The band that summer was the Ted Huston orchestra. Ted played the piano and the other members of the band played clarinet/saxophone, bass violin, drums, and the accordion.

Ted and his family had rooms in the hotel and two members of the band were local musicians. The remaining band members rented rooms in town.

Chapter 20

A Change Of Plans

In the summer of 1958, I was engage to my high school sweetheart. We were both in college, separate ones, studying to be teachers and life was moving along as we had planned.

At one time I had thought of becoming a nurse but Mother had other plans. During the past winter I learned about the field of music therapy and that intrigued me. I visited the V A Hospital in Indianapolis and saw how music could actually help heal and planned to possibly pursue that field of study as a minor when I returned to I U in the fall. But plans were all about to change.

The Right Place at the Right Time

The circumstances that placed me at the French Lick Sheraton Hotel in 1958, had their beginning when I was just five and a half years old and didn't want to go to school.

A child had to be six years old before January 1st in order to start first grade in September. I had only missed the deadline by one week. Tom Taggart, Jr. had offered to use his influence to get me accepted if my parents wanted me to start. My mother told me that when she and Daddy asked me, I said that I didn't want to go to school. They thought I meant not that year, but I meant I never wanted to go to school. I was perfectly happy to wallow in ignorance for the rest of my life. My mother wasn't about to let that happen.

We had this big, tall piano in the dining room that I, in all innocence, never imagining where it could lead, tried out the keys to just see what they felt like. That was all that Mother needed to decide that I was a budding pianist just waiting to bloom. Besides, people would look at my long fingers and say things like, "Those long fingers were meant to play the piano." Kind of like the way people assume that if you are tall you should play basketball. So Mother started me with lessons when I was five and a half from our church pianist, Nancy Clay, who was still in high school. If I wasn't going to school then I was going to learn something.

Nancy didn't seem anymore thrilled about teaching than I was about learning. She was usually still in bed when I arrived for my lesson.

At my first lesson Nancy had me tap each finger on her dining room table. Then I sat at the piano with both thumbs on middle C. I figured I had learned enough. Mother didn't. Nancy soon found that we both preferred for her to play the piano and for me to sing. After Nancy went away to college I thought I was free but Mother found another teacher, Mrs. McIntosh.

Mrs. McIntosh lived just on the other side of our next door neighbors, the Porters. All I remember about those lessons was that her house was dark inside and I was scared of her. I also made sure I didn't learn anything. When she died I again thought I was free but Mother found Mrs. Lula Pruitt.

Mrs. Pruitt lived a block away and by now I really hated going to lessons. Sometimes I would hide my lesson book in the bushes in front of her house, knock on her door, and tell her I couldn't find my book. Then I would go home and tell Mother that Mrs. Pruitt wasn't home. I cannot tell you enough how much I hated piano lessons but Mother would say to me, "You'll thank me someday." When Mrs. Pruitt died I again thought I was free. Wrong. I never could figure out how my mother could keep coming up with piano teachers in such a small town.

My strong dislike of piano lessons really was not directed at the teacher personally but the way my teachers kept dropping like flies was beginning to look suspicious, after all, I did have motive. Although nothing was ever proven I remained a "person of interest" for years.

After the passing of Mrs. Pruitt there was a brief lull when I didn't take lessons. I think teachers may have been leery of taking me on as a student. But finally, Mother persuaded Jessie Dickey to take me as a pupil.

Mrs. Dickey taught me to play "Glow Little Glow Worm" by ear, then she switched to her playing the piano and me singing, much like my first piano teacher had done. Perhaps that was the secret to breaking the hex.

When our church organist got married the church was in need of another organist. The very idea of hiring an organist was unheard of. It was many years later that I found out that some churches actually *paid* musicians to play for church. Nancy Thurston and I had both taken piano lessons and since we were members of the church they wouldn't have to pay us. Nancy was very good and I was mediocre. Nevertheless, both of us were sent to take organ lessons so we could take over the church duties. I actually enjoyed those lessons. That teacher survived.

It was through my organ teacher that I began taking voice lessons from Anna Kaskas in her studio at Indiana University while I was a senior in high school. I'm not sure how he arranged it but before I knew what was happening, I was being auditioned by Ms. Kaskas who had been a member of the Metropolitan Opera Company. She accepted me as a student and began my studies, preparing me for my entrance into the university. I discovered that singing required so much more than vocal cords; it required mind, body, and spirit. I discovered that every muscle in my body was part of this instrument that produced singing. I found that I really enjoyed singing arias even though I had never seen an opera.

Through the years, the Taggart family had maintained a relationship with my father so when I was preparing to graduate from high school, Miss Lucy Taggart gave me two tickets to a performance of the Metropolitan Opera at Indiana University.

That night I saw my first opera and this little "Hick from French Lick" (Larry Bird isn't the only one who can claim that title) heard magic. The opera was sung in Italian and we had the libretto but I really didn't need to refer to it. The words of the arias were not that important. I simply thrilled to hear the beauty of the human voice as the singers sang their arias. Some people think opera singers are 'putting-on', but in fact they are simply opening their instrument, supporting the tone with controlled air, and letting the sound flow out in its purest form.

In September I entered Indiana University as a music education major. I had no-none-zero preparation in music theory; those 'good boys' and 'grass-eating cows' hadn't helped me at all. But in my first semester of theory I learned the evolution of musical notation. I learned that the treble clef was actually a fancy G that hooked around the line that holds G above middle C. The bass clef was really a fancy F showing where F below middle C is and there is really only one line separating the treble lines from the bass lines. By saying the musical alphabet, which only has seven letters, forward and backward, it is easy to know the names if the notes. I learned about intervals, chord construction, sight singing; so many basic things that no one had bothered to explain to me. In other words, I learned the language of music. I even began to enjoy my piano lessons at the university and wanted to spread the gospel of theory.

Johnny's journey to the French Lick Sheraton Hotel also had its beginning when he was only five and a half years old.

Unlike me, Johnny's first love **was** the piano. He had made his debut on a stage when he was in the first grade. His brother Frank, who was five years older than Johnny, and some of Frank's friends had a band and were entertaining at their school. They carried a small coffin onto the stage, sat

121

it down, and out popped little five year old Johnny, dressed in a tuxedo, who sat down at the grand piano and performed with the group.

Johnny loved the piano but his father had been a professional accordionist and wanted Johnny to play that instrument. In fact, both of Johnny's older brothers also played the accordion so the die had been cast.

Johnny was enrolled as a student of Professor Fred Hofstadter, a highly respected teacher of accordion in the Toledo area.

Johnny went on to be an award-winning accordionist and played in several different bands in the Toledo area.

Friends of Frankie Yankovic, "The Polka King", took Johnny to audition for his polka band that was playing in Detroit. Just a couple of days after that, another musician friend told Johnny of an opening with the Ted Huston Orchestra that was playing at a hotel in Toledo. These two bands were well-known but played different styles of music; Yankovic's was a polka band that traveled extensively throughout the United States, doing mostly one-night stands and Huston's band played what was termed 'society music' and had longer engagements in hotels. Johnny audition for the Ted Huston Orchestra and was offered that job also. Both bands were excellent opportunities for a young accordionist. Johnny accepted Ted Huston's offer and that decision led to our future.

When Ted told him where they would be going it isn't surprising that Johnny asked, "Where is French Lick, Indiana?" He had no idea where he was going....or what he was getting into.

When Johnny first arrived in French Lick, that city kid immediately felt something akin to awe, never expecting such grandeur after all the twists and turns of the narrow road that took him to the remote valley of French Lick.

The band didn't usually start work until dinner time at the hotel, so during the day the band members would mingle with the town's people. Johnny felt an atmosphere of kindness and friendliness from the people he met that endeared him forever to the small town of French Lick.

The band was allowed to eat their meals at the hotel so when the three bachelor bandsmen came to the hotel, they would often stop at my desk to say "hello".

After our first meeting in June, Johnny and I would sometimes sit on the front porch of the hotel during the half hour between my getting off work and Johnny starting his evening, playing with the band for dinner in the dining room, followed with playing for dancing in the lobby.

I began to realize that I had feelings for this young man from Toledo, Ohio, feelings that were not just a physical attraction. Oh yes, those were definitely there, but there was an attraction that was something different, something I couldn't explain.

Johnny was just beginning the next big step in his career as a musician. But I believe that God had planned for us to share our lives. Now don't think for a minute that because God brings two people together that their lives are meant to be trouble free. Neither of us had any idea what our future together would be, but looking back on the 57 years we were together I can see *some* of God's plans. For what I do not understand, well, as the hymnist says, "Farther along we'll know all about it, farther along we'll understand why".

Because Johnny worked seven nights a week, we never had a real date. Eventually Johnny had asked if he could come to our house after work to visit me. It was around midnight before he got off work so I needed my mother's permission (I was only twenty) to have a visitor that late. We would sit in the kitchen and drink coffee or go out in the back yard and in the midnight moonlight and amid the chorus of crickets we shared our life stories and our hopes for the future. I had no idea where this was going to lead but I did know that I was feeling something for Johnny that I had never felt before.

With all of this going on inside my heart I knew that I could not continue in my engagement. I returned my engagement ring and said goodbye to the dear sweetheart of my youth and the future we had planned. I now faced an uncertain future but one that I felt was planned by God.

~

In August Johnny invited me to a party he was hosting for the band and their wives. It was at this party that he gave me a present, saying it was for my birthday. I told him, "My birthday is in January." And he said that he had missed it so this was a belated birthday present. When I open the box there was a skirt, two sizes too big, and secretly I wondered if he thought I was *that* big. But when I lifted the skirt out of the box there was a much smaller box lying there among the tissue paper. He told me to open it and when I did, I saw an engagement ring. That is when and how he asked me to marry him and to save him any embarrassment in front of his friends I said, "YES". (That's my story and I'm sticking to it.) Incidentally, he had borrowed that skirt from the wife of one of the guys in the band. Today that skirt would fit me.

We become engaged that Saturday night in August and on Monday Johnny was fired by his boss, Ted Huston. Sheraton had a rule that there could be no "fraternizing" among the "help" and Johnny had apparently been "fraternizing". Johnny just went directly to the General Manager and stated his case against being fired. Johnny was rehired immediately.

I learned early on that Johnny was not afraid to speak up for what he felt was right. I think that Ted had reacted so quickly because he was afraid that my father, Frank McDonald, would not approve. Daddy was a formidable person, but, with his sense of propriety, Johnny had gone to my father to tell him his intentions and asked his permission to marry me. Johnny told my father that he was not only a musician but a machinist. As it happened, that evening my sister, Vi, called and my mother overheard Daddy telling her, "Eva is getting married to a boy she met in the hotel's band but he's also a machinist." Maybe that had been Johnny's saving grace; Daddy was apparently impressed that Johnny was not only a musician but was skilled in a trade. My mother and little brother hid in the bathroom when

Johnny showed up at our house to talk to my father. I'm not sure what they thought would happen, I didn't know either, however, to my relief and great surprise, Daddy just said, "It's her life." I never knew that.

Thinking back to that summer I can see that my father really wasn't so blind-sided by the appearance of Johnny into my life. My father's sleeping porch was very near where we would sit in the back yard and I'm sure he could hear every word we were saying. Daddy never slept straight through the night. He always woke up about every two hours, would read until he got sleepy again and repeat this cycle. It never occurred to me at the time that he was probably hearing every word we were saying.

chapter 21

By Candlelight At Twilight

That wonderful summer of 1958 had turned to autumn when on October 3rd, 1958, at a candlelight service in the little church I attended, Johnny Kobee and I became Mr. and Mrs. The reception was held in the church basement. Our beautiful cake was created by Jim Leonard, the master baker at the hotel, and all of our flowers came from the hotel's greenhouse. We were married 57 years before Johnny entered into his eternal rest with our Lord and Savior, Jesus Christ. We have 3 children, 8 grandchildren, and so far there are 9 great-grandchildren and I am looking forward to more additions, (hint, hint).

Ted told us that from French Lick we would be going to Washington, D.C. and he and his wife showed us pictures of where they would be staying and suggested where we should live. However, on October 31st the Ted Huston Orchestra finished their season at the French Lick Sheraton and Ted announced that we would be going to Louisville, Kentucky. So Washington D.C. was out. We came back to the French Lick Sheraton to play for the New Year's Eve party and Johnny got fired, again.

After the official celebration ended the band played for a private party in the penthouse. Some of the guys were feeling no pain, including the leader, Ted. Johnny was the only one who had not joined in the drinking and neither had I. We had just learned that I was pregnant and besides, I wasn't old enough to drink alcohol. After the penthouse party, Ted and his wife, Lee, invited us to their suite. While we were talking to Lee, Ted was in the other room and something was said that he misunderstood and he came in the room and said to Johnny, "You're fired." This was becoming a reoccurring theme and we didn't take it seriously. The next day Ted called Johnny and apologized, recanting the firing.

We were staying with my parents that night and walked home, hand in hand, in the predawn hours of this, our first New Year's morning together. We got home around 4 A.M. and my father was already up, fixing his breakfast in the kitchen. Johnny whispered to me, "Don't you want to go wish you dad, 'Happy New Year'?" I whispered back, "No." and quickly went into our bedroom. I had *never* come home in the wee hours of the morning before and the little girl in me was afraid to face my Daddy.

While we were in Louisville, Ted had told the band that they would be spending the winter playing at a hotel in Miami, but in fact we headed the opposite direction to Buffalo, NY and we stayed there the entire winter.

Just before that engagement was over, Ted told the band that they would be moving to New York City but, again, that suddenly changed to the Air Force Base at Goose Bay, Labrador, Canada, and wives could not go.

Ted seemed to have a serious problem with direction (and truth), so we decided it was time to go in our own direction. Johnny gave Ted his notice and as the band headed to Canada we headed back to French Lick, Indiana to await the arrival of our first baby.

On the way back to French Lick we stopped in Waterville, Ohio to visit with Johnny's parent for a few days. We happened to be in the village on Memorial Day and saw the high school's band, The Anthony Wayne Marching Generals, lead the parade of veterans and Boy Scouts and Girl Scouts to the Maumee River. The Women's Axillary of the American Legion placed wreaths in the river to pay homage to those lost at sea and there was a gun salute followed by taps being played. Then the parade moved to the village cemetery where speeches were given, and the members of the military that had fallen on land were remembered. We were so impressed with the patriotism of the community exhibited here in this village that we both began to think that we might like to live in such a town. Here again God seemed to be placing a desire in each of our hearts.

~

During this time when we were not sure where our future lay we stayed with me parents in French Lick to await the arrival of our first child, Julia Elizabeth, who was born on July 21, 1959.

Johnny worked at the hotel during the Jazz Festival and played in a band on the week-ends at the American Legion in Jasper.

In late August a telephone call came from Johnny's brother, Frank. He was opening a machine shop in Toledo, something to do with plastic molds, and he wanted Johnny to come and work for him. Johnny felt it was his family duty to help his brother in this endeavor so in September we packed up our things and headed back to Waterville, Ohio. Almost everything we owned fit in our Pontiac that we had bought with our wedding money the year before. The one thing that didn't make it into the car was the beautiful chifferobe Johnny had built for Julie while we were at my parents' home; so we sent it by train from the depot in French Lick to the depot in Waterville.

Johnny's parents invited us to stay with them until we could find suitable housing for our little family.

~

Remembering how we had liked the village of Waterville, we decided to make that our home for the time being. For me Waterville was just a temporary home because I wanted us to settle in French Lick. This "temporary" home turned out to be where we spent the next 40 years.

During my first winter in Ohio, Julie and I lived with Johnny's parents. I say Julie and I because Johnny was hardly ever there. He left very early every morning, carrying his packed lunch and thermos of coffee, and dragged home very late at night having not had any supper. On some nights he would work all night – again no supper – helping Frank get a job done that was unrealistically promised by Frank.

Johnny took me on a tour of the shop where he was working and attempted to explain all the machines to me. I nodded and tried to act like I understood but I really had no clue. As days turned into weeks and months and years I saw my hope of returning to French Lick being put on hold; delayed but not forgotten – never forgotten.

We began to see payroll not being met at the time expected, and then one day Johnny returned home within an hour after leaving for work because the IRS had padlocked the business. This was right after Christmas and the employees' paychecks had bounced, leaving us high and dry and in debt.

With a growing family to support, Johnny quickly applied at Sears and was hired as a salesman in the tire department.

But before Frank's shop closed, Johnny had met a musician who lived next to the shop, Jim Gottron, who was also a piano tuner-technician. Johnny became intrigued with piano tuning and Jim started teaching him the art. With Johnny's ear for correct pitch, his manual skills and attention to detail, he was a natural. Eventually a large music store in Toledo where Jim sometimes tuned needed another fulltime piano tuner and Jim recommended Johnny for the job.

In 1977 Johnny decided it was time for him to go on his own, so Kobee's Piano Service was born.

For the first couple of years Kobee's Piano Service was a home-based business. I took care of answering the phone and making appointments for tunings. Johnny would bring home piano actions that needed repairing and our dining room table became his work table.

Before long it became apparent that Johnny needed an actual workshop so we rented a place that was big enough to have a workshop and could also accommodate a show room for pianos. We began buying used pianos and Johnny would rebuild them and sell them. His business was really growing. That was when we decided that I would join him full time at the shop. I became his "gofer" or helper, not really a new job for me; I had been a gofer with many,....wait,.... make that ALL of his projects at home.

~

One time will never be forgotten: I became a "golden gofer".

We were just finishing painting our home harvest gold and Johnny noticed a spot that had been missed. He asked me to hold the ladder while he climbed up to paint the missed spot. As he started to ascend the ladder he was carrying a paint brush in one hand and a full gallon of harvest gold paint in the other. I suggested he just put a little paint in a small bucket but, no, this was faster; he always knew best. Up he went. He hung the full gallon of harvest gold paint on an 'S' hook before stepping off of the ladder to the roof near the missed spot. After painting the spot, he stepped back to the ladder and his foot bumped the 'S' hook. The gallon of paint landed, smack on its bottom, on the ground between the house and the ladder, and the paint sprang up, out of the can, and landed on me. I was solid gold from the top of my head to the bottom of my shoes. Even my underwear was soaked with harvest gold paint. Johnny stood on that ladder looking down at my gold hair, gold face, and gold body; he didn't move or say a word. Our sons, John and Jeff, were standing as still as statues, eyes fixed, taking in what must have looked like a scene from the Three Stooges. I only remember an eerie silence; even the birds stopped singing.

I spoke first and simply said, "Very funny".

I think I heard a sigh from my menfolk as I sloshed into the house to start the cleanup.

My daughter, Julie, wanted to take my picture but I was not in the mood. Fortunately, the paint was latex which is water soluble so what I could not peel off I could wash off. I pitched the clothes and shoes.

~

With Kobee's Piano Service now having a shop, I would spend my days there, helping Johnny when he was working on a piano action and answering phones when he was out tuning pianos. When Johnny would be out of the shop I started envisioning a music store in conjunction with the piano showroom. I shared that idea and Johnny agreed that this could be a good thing. But he thought that I shouldn't teach, just stock the lesson books for the other teachers in the area. I agreed. I had been teaching piano for a long time but I hadn't found it to be as fulfilling as I felt it should be.

My first step was to canvas all of the teachers nearby and ask what books they would like for me to stock. Then I proceeded to bring in music that they would be using. I also stocked a few accessories for band instruments: reeds, drum sticks, etc. plus guitar strings and picks, small items that people might need. I also contacted Abby Press and stocked music related gifts and greeting cards. The "store" was just a corner of the room but gave me something to do when not needed in the shop.

That is when I came across the Alfred lesson books and my interest in teaching was rekindled. This was the beginning of the most rewarding time of teaching music I had ever known. I was not so much a 'piano' teacher but a teacher who taught 'music via the piano'.

My student enrollment quickly grew from 1 student in October to 30 students who played at our recital in June. Within ten years I was teaching between 50 and 70 students weekly with extra theory classes on Saturday. The ages of the students ranged from 4 to 65 years old. I became certified as a private piano teacher by the Ohio Music Teachers Association and was a member of the Toledo Piano Teachers Organization.

At one of our recitals my mother was visiting and at the final bow, I stood on the stage and with a lump the size of a baseball in my throat, honestly and publicly said to my mother, "Thank you."

When our son Jeff was a junior in high school, he came home one day and said that the teacher who was directing the music for the high school's musical, *Dear World*, based on the play, *The Madwoman of Chaillot*, was ill and could not continue as the music director. Jeff had volunteered me for the job. That sounded very exciting to me so I agreed to take over the job. Now I was able to use all of my training in music education: theory, voice, and multiple instrument technics. The instrumentation was for an orchestra and we had a band, albeit a good one, but I had to transpose some of the music to fit our instruments in the pit orchestra. The setting for the play was Paris, France, so Johnny joined the orchestra and added the French flavor to the music with his accordion. Jeff was cast as a juggler and taught himself to juggle, something he had never done before. Now this play had become a family affair.

There was a runway built around the pit orchestra and we in the pit became the river Seine. One night during a break at rehearsal, some of the kids were jumping over the orchestra pit. Jeff started to do the same and as he took a springing position, he caught my eye and silently mouthed, "Is it ok?" I silently mouthed, "We don't have insurance." Jeff just turned around and walked away....Jeff has always had a good head on his shoulders.

Being self-employed isn't all it is cracked up to be. For one thing, buying our own medical insurance was financially prohibitive. So after ten wonderful years of teaching in my own studio, and loving every minute of it, we decided to close our shop/studio and I would find a job that offered medical insurance.

I sadly "retired" from teaching and began looking for a full-time job with benefits. We only had one car and Johnny's piano tuning business was keeping him busy tuning pianos in homes, churches and schools as far as 75 miles away, so I needed to be able to walk to work. There was only one place in Waterville that might meet my two requirements, benefits and within walking distance, and that was Arbors at Waterville Nursing Center, which was about a quarter of a mile from our home. Finally, on a warm, late summer day, I dressed in a blue cotton skirt and a white cotton blouse, and as I brushed my hair and finished preparing to go to Arbors, I cried. A Nursing Home was the LAST place on earth where I wanted to work…but I needed a job so I put "need" ahead of "want" and walked down the edge of the Anthony Wayne Trail and up the hill to the front door of Arbors.

The only opening they had was for a 'dietary aide', which is a euphemism for 'dishwasher'. Not the job I would have liked but I would get medical insurance for my family and that is what I needed. I accepted the position.

By the end of my eight hour days of working on a brick floor, my back hurt so much that when I got home and could finally sit down I could not stand up again without help. My back never got use to the pain but I think I just got mad enough that I decided that job WAS NOT GOING TO BEAT ME: I would do it or die trying.

But before I died the Dietary Clerk position became available.

The reason that the clerk position became available was because our department was switching to having our menus and dietary requirements entered into a computer. Many of the staff were not thrilled with the change and were even threatening to quit if they had to learn 'computer'. I can't say why but I really WANTED to learn 'computer'. I got the job. Now I was a dietary aide three days a week and dietary clerk two days and I got to sit down, occasionally, on those two days. A few months later I was offered the job as a cook.

I am not a cook; never learned how. Mother said I would just 'know' how when the time came. She was wrong. I still don't know the fine art of cooking. I can cook, but it is very plain and basic, nothing with flair or creativity, that was Johnny's talent. But the meals and their preparations at the nursing facility were so well-regulated that all I had to do was follow the recipes. Creativity was frowned upon. I took great pride in being a cook but it was taking a toll on my health.

Then the day came when the receptionist was going to be away from the facility for a while and I volunteered to cover the front desk during my lunch hour, answering phones and greeting people. After that initial offer on my part, when the office manager needed someone to fill in as receptionist I was asked to do that job. Later when that position became available full time, the manager who had seen that I could handle multiple telephone lines offered me the position. FINALLY, I could sit down to work, wear regular clothes, and have week-ends and holidays off.

I enjoyed my new duties and the pay was better. I imagined being at Arbors until I retired, but, again the direction of my life changed. In fact, life took a U-turn, pointing me back to French Lick, Indiana.

Chapter 22

Full Circle

In early spring of 2000 I met the man in charge of hiring entertainment for the hotel. I asked him if he was looking for someone to play piano and he said, "Do you know of someone?"

I answered, "Yes, my husband." He asked me to send Johnny in to meet him the very next day.

Johnny auditioned on the piano in the lobby and was hired on the spot. His first "gig" was playing at the Arts Festival that was held in the former convention hall, now called the Grand Colonnade Ball Room. Besides exhibiting beautiful art work, other musicians were asked to play during the Festival and our family was well represented. The music teacher at the high school volunteered our granddaughter, Tabitha, who was already an accomplished trumpet player at the age of 15, to be on the program.

Johnny was also hired to play every Saturday for afternoon tea in the lobby and Sunday morning brunch in the main dining room. Eventually, Johnny was also playing in the evenings on the weekends at the hotel's Jack's Steakhouse. At last, Johnny was seeing his dream being fulfilled.

Soon Johnny was playing for many different events and he was also tuning the various pianos in the hotel for a variety of performers who appeared at the hotel such as the revived Big Bands: The Duke Ellington, Guy

Lombardo, and Glen Miller Bands. One happy piano player who had performed at the hotel several times in the past even gave a big "Thank You, to Johnny Kobee" at the dance, saying it was the finest tuning that piano had ever had.

Johnny was also being asked to play for many of the wedding receptions held at the hotel. When the wedding couple would hear Johnny play, I loved to see the way their eyes would grow misty with the romance that he would bring to his music.

Sometimes a couple would want music for the wedding ceremony and since I had a classical background and had played the organ for many weddings in my church I would get to play for the actual ceremony. Our wonderful electric keyboard had the capacity to sound like many different instruments including a church organ.

Many weddings were held in the garden around the pond. The Bridal party often chose to stand at the top of the waterfall for the service, that way all of the family and friends could easily see the couple as they spoke their vows. For safety's sake the bride would usually walk barefoot up the little hill to stand beside the groom and exchange their marriage vows.

One wedding I will never forget took place on St. Valentine's Day. The couple came in that day with no pre-planning beyond having a license. They asked if I could find a Minister or Justice of the Peace to perform the ceremony. I was able to find one who, believe it or not, was named Elvis. The bride was adamant that the ceremony be held in the garden. Ordinarily that would be a good choice but this was February 14. Besides being cold, a light rain had been falling all day. The couple had not brought witnesses for the wedding so the bride asked the wife of the minister to be her maid-of-honor. The groom said he would really like to have the concierge as part of the wedding so I got to be his best-'man'. I was truly honored to have that job: this was the first time, ever, that I got to be in a wedding party, other than my own of course. So there we stood in the garden-facing the pond-in the cold, drizzle-on St. Valentin's Day-with Elvis performing the ceremony….how cool is that?

One day our General Manager came to the lobby and laid a letter he had received on my desk and said, "A-va', see what we can do for zeese people'". I have to admit that every time I repeated something that Dominic said I involuntarily went into a very poor French accent. On reading the letter I learned that Mr. Palmer had met his wife in November of 1948 while they were students in high school attending a High School Journalist Conference at the French Lick Springs Hotel. They were from different high schools in the Minneapolis area and had met on the train coming to French Lick. He said they spent the days walking the grounds at the Resort, skipping most of the conference sessions unless they had a mutual reason to attend one, danced the nights away in the French Lick Ballroom, and ended up marrying two years later. The Palmers now lived in California but were coming to the French Lick Springs Hotel soon. Mr. Palmer said he didn't remember which room he had been in but he remembered that it had a slanting floor and hoped we hadn't corrected the slant...it had given the room character that he had never forgotten. He wondered if they could possibly have the same room. I reported to Dominic that they had two important memories of the hotel: a room with a slanting floor, and dancing in the lobby.

At that time in 2000, the hotel had several rooms with floors that slanted to varying degrees and Dominic had the front desk put them in the room with the most slanting floor of all the rooms.

As for dancing, we no longer had a hotel orchestra but M. Audran suggested having a piano moved into Jacks Steakhouse and Johnny play for them during dinner.

After dinner, Johnny offered to play the piano in the lobby so they could once again "dance the night away". They were delighted. Mrs. Palmer, an excellent musician, had brought her flute to the hotel and joined Johnny in some duets. The Palmers were very good dancers and we referred to them as "Fred and Ginger". This was an evening that Johnny and I treasured.

When ITT acquired the Sheraton Corporation in 1968, they determined that the older hotels in the chain were not what they wanted so they began selling their older properties. In spite of being very profitable, the French Lick Sheraton was sold to the Cox Hotel Corporation of New York in 1979.

Very little was put into the hotel by Cox. About all that was done was remodeling the convention hall, slapping some paint here and there, and changing the name of the property to the French Lick Springs Golf and Tennis Resort.

Around this time Norman Rales from Maryland, bought some of the property behind the hotel where the hotel's dairy had once been and built the French Lick Villas.

In the 1980's, people would be invited to stay at the French Lick Springs Golf and Tennis Resort for a week-end that included a tour of the hotel and a sales pitch for buying a timeshare in the new Villas. One of the appeals of the villas was the close proximity of the hotel and its amenities: pool, tennis courts, golf, restaurants, etc., all of which were available to Villa guests.

The hotel continued to operate in spite of the neglect of the building. Faithfull employees did all that they could to made the guests comfortable and their stay enjoyable but Hoosier Hospitality can only go so far in an old hotel that is looking more and more shabby.

In 1986, the hotel again was sold, this time to Kenwood Financial, headed by Norman Rales. But as had been the case with Cox, Rales was not interested in putting money into the much-needed repairs to the hotel especially the 'back of the house'. Rales' agenda was to sell timeshares in his villas.

For some reason, the salespeople pitching the villas thought it necessary to embellish the history of the hotel. As they would be taking guests through the hotel, staff members who overheard these 'historical' facts often found them to be down-right 'hysterical', and had a hard time keeping a straight face. But these stories came back to haunt me when I gave the history tour of the hotel, starting with.....

Ghosts

The sixth floor was a place where folks who believe in ghosts say they have seen them. The older Taggarts lived on that floor and their suite was connected to the suite below where the younger Taggarts lived. Until the renovation of the hotel in 2006 these two suites were called the Presidential and Governors Suites.

Personally, I am skeptical when it comes to "ghosts" at the hotel. Maybe that is because the past at the hotel is not so far in the past to me. Knowing that my father was working at the hotel when it was being built by Mr. Taggart makes it seem too new to have "ghosts". However, there are some very trustworthy folks who swear that they have not only seen "ghost" but have taken pictures of them. One member of the security staff said that when the hotel closed and was being restored these spirits were very active. So I must agree with Hamlet and say, "There are more things in Heaven and Earth, Horatio, than are dreamt of in your philosophy."

Jail

Off of the hall that once led to all the workshops was a room with a window in the door with bars in it. This had been pointed out by the salespeople of the timeshares that the room had once been used as a jail. Because I couldn't find any records to back that up I asked the Chief Engineer, Don Qualkenbush, if it had ever been a jail. He scoffed at the idea and said the bars were on the door for ventilation. They stored paint in there. However as I was digging around in the various histories of the French Lick valley I did find a story about some outlaws known as the Archer Gang who had been confined briefly in the French Lick Hotel, awaiting being taken to the county jail in Paoli, but that would have been prior to 1886, the year when the gang's activities were terminated in a lynching, a quarter of a century before the wing in question was added.

As a Halloween activity around 2004, the hotel welcomed some ghost finders to the hotel and they reported seeing the ghosts of men sitting in the 'jail' playing cards. Maybe that was where one of the casinos had been.

The Clairvoyant

A lady who claimed to be a clairvoyant once stayed at our hotel. Before she left she asked me if we could talk about ghostly happenings at the hotel. I warned her that I had no personal experience along those lines, only things that I had heard from other people. I know there has been a book written about ghosts in Indiana and the French Lick Hotel was included as a ghost-location. As I have said, I do not believe in 'ghosts', but I do believe in the spirit world. Is there a difference? To me there is. I believe there are evil spirits and I most definitely believe in Holy Angels because I have seen their work. I believe in the Holy Spirit, the third person of the Holy Trinity. I believe that when a Christian passes from this life their soul and spirit passes into the presence of Jesus Christ. Just how all of this is done I do not know and I do not worry about it. God is in charge and I am not God.

The clairvoyant was especially interested in sightings of members of the Taggart family. When I asked her what room she had been staying in, she said it was a suite at the end of the fifth floor, The Governor's Suite. I told her that she had been staying in the former residence of the Tom Taggart, Jr.'s family. I didn't say it, but I wondered, "Why hadn't she known that?"

The Seventh Floor

On Sunday mornings when most of our guests were checking out I would help the bellmen by standing at their desk, answer their phone and take requests for assistance with their luggage. One Sunday morning when I was helping out at the bellmen's stand a man approached me and asked, "When do you do the tour of the seventh floor?" This caught me off guard and without thinking I said, "Why would I give a tour of the seventh floor?" He then informed me that the seventh floor was where all the gangsters had stayed and he had been on that tour several years before. I saw this as a teaching moment (I do that a lot) and proceeded to tell him that gangsters probably never stayed at the French Lick Springs Hotel, at least not to anyone's knowledge. I did say that the seventh floor had been used by some of the Republican Governors who gathered here in 1971 but I wasn't sure if that counted.

Tunnel Vision

I suspect that was the same tour that showed guests a door on the lower level of the hotel, under the hall leading to the spa that supposedly opened to a tunnel leading to the West Baden Hotel. Folks were told that the gangsters, i.e. Al Capone and company, would crawl through that tunnel from one hotel to the other to avoid the "Feds". I enjoyed bursting the bubble of unbelievable fairy tales and telling the REAL stories that, in truth, were much more interesting.

If you are interested in finding where that so-called tunnel was, it is now the passage way below the first floor that leads to the Recreation Center from the lowest entrance at the front of the hotel. Of course, until the restoration of the hotel in 2005-2006, that passage way was nothing but a crawl space, barely large enough for a man to get through in order to check the pipes that ran through it.

The Gangster's Honeymoon

One story that has been told so often that in the repeated telling seems to have become 'fact' is that Al Capone came to the valley on his honeymoon and when he and his wedding party came to the French Lick Hotel, Tom Taggart, Sr., stopped him at the front door and would not let him in. I do not doubt that Tom Taggart would have turned Al Capone away. This hotel and Taggart's position in the political world were second only to his family in importance and welcoming "Scarface" to his hotel would have been out of the question. The part I am certain to be incorrect is that Capone was on his honeymoon. Capone married is wife, Mae Josephine Coughlin, in New York on December 30, 1918 when he was just 20 years old and was living in Brooklyn, New York. He didn't make his mark with the Chicago mob until he moved to Chicago in 1919 with his wife and son.

I think there may have been a mix up in gangsters and their honeymoons. "Big" Jim Colosimo, did spend his honeymoon with Dale Winters, his second wife, in a home in French Lick in 1920. Just two weeks after the newlyweds returned to Chicago, "Big Jim" Colosimo was murdered by a faction of the Chicago Mob, likely by Al Capone.

Ferdinand, Indiana

There is a little town just 44 miles southwest of French Lick named Ferdinand. On the top of the town's hill stands the Monastery Immaculate Conception, home to one of the largest communities of Benedictine women in the United States. When I was the concierge at the hotel I often encouraged guests to visit this beautiful Monastery.

The town holds a Christmas event each year and the French Lick Springs Hotel would sometimes donate the trolley and a driver to carry visitors around the town of Ferdinand while one of their guides gave a history tour. It was from that tour that I learned of a cottage industry that connected Chicago, Illinois, to Ferdinand, Indiana.

It seems that this innocent-looking little town of around 2,000 souls, had the best quality moonshine made during prohibition. They claim that Capone appreciated the fact that the local Germans never cut the moonshine with lye and that he purchased whiskey that was sent by rail to Speakeasy's in Chicago.

Historic Landmark boasts that Al Capone was a guest at the West Baden Hotel on more than one occasion. My personal belief is that Al Capone and other gangsters did come to French Lick/West Baden. Where gossip is prevalent there is often a grain of truth and with so many stories about 'bad boys' coming to the valley, there too is probably a grain of truth. Near the Gorge Super Club is a house where it is also rumored that Capone stayed. That to me would make more sense because of it being a more private place.

Stories are also told about John Dillinger passing through West Baden, stopping at a gas station for a fill-up, and handing the owner a $100 dollar bill as he and his gang sped off. Sounds plausible.

The Ballard Boys

The Gorge "Supper Club" was located just a few miles from the town of French Lick and in a very secluded…Gorge, of course. It was run by Ed Ballard's brother, Joe Ballard. One of the safety features of that casino was that the two-lane road entering the Gorge property ran under a stone arch becoming a one-lane road, limiting the entrance and being able to block any unwanted cars from approaching the building. A local historians told me that when the state police stormed down on the valley for the final raid that closed the casino in 1950, they approached the Gorge from the back by climbing over a hill and down to the ravine, out of sight of the guards that stood on watchtowers at the front entrance to the Gorge.

This building was eventually turned into a nursing home and some of the old-timers living there swore there were tunnels under the building, where, in the event of a raid, patrons and equipment could disappear. The closest thing I have ever seen to a "tunnel" is one of the many small caves that are in the hills around the valley. I have also been in a coal mine not far from French Lick. With limestone, sandstone, shale and coal under the soil, I find it hard to imagine all the digging and blasting it would take to make some of the "tunnels".

The Mackinac Island Connection.

One evening I was helping in Jack's Steakhouse as hostess when I met Bob Tagatz, the resident historian of Grand Hotel. This was in the winter when the Grand Hotel was closed. Mr. Tagatz filled me in on some of the history of the Grand that related to the French Lick/West Baden Springs.

Through Mr. Tagatz I learned that the Grand Hotel had once been owned by members of the Ballard family beginning with J. Logan Ballard in 1918.

When J. Logan Ballard died in 1923, the Grand went into the Ballard Estate and eventually to Ed Ballard. By 1925 Joe Ballard had entered into a partnership with two other men with the understanding that Joe could have his own gambling club at the Grand. Joe Ballard died three months after the stock market crash of 1929 putting the Grand back into the Ballard Estate Trust and was put up for auction in 1933.

I had heard the name Mackinac Island from as far back as I could remember. It was a place where some of my mother's brothers would go in the summer to work, driving carriages. I always wondered where this place was and why didn't I ever get to go there. I thought it must just be a place where only young men went.

With the Ballard family being involved with the Grand Hotel, people from French Lick and West Baden Springs who needed employment were encouraged to go to Mackinac Island in the summers to work. Some worked in the hotel and others had various jobs on the island, including driving the horse drawn carriages. My uncle Duke was one of the carriage drivers when he was still in his teens. Years later, Uncle Duke took his family to Mackinac Island for a vacation and met drivers he had worked with many years before. They suggested that he come back during his vacation the next year and drive carriages. Uncle Duke took them up on the idea and he and his family started spending every vacation thereafter at the Island. They bought a home on the Island where they stayed in the summer and Uncle Duke, after retiring from his job as a truck driver, stayed on the Island through the winters. He even was elected to the city council on Mackinac Island. Uncle Duke was so happy to have been one of the drivers who carried Jane Seymour around on the Island when she was there making the movie, *Somewhere In Time*. He said she was always very kind and pleasant and very beautiful. When he had to retire from driving horses due to ill health, he was given a pair of Percheron horses that he named "Duke" and "Rosie" after himself and his wife, Aunt Rosemary.

Mr. Tagatz also told me that during prohibition The Grand Hotel, like so many other establishments, made money through offering liquor and gambling to those who sought it. Professional gamblers could rent a large suite for $15,000 a year to be used as a gambling club room or "speakeasy". Home-grown whiskey was made and sold on the island.

Bob told me that the Grand was never raided, unless it wanted to be. When things were a little slow, a call to the Michigan State Police reporting gambling and alcohol at the Grand Hotel would result in a raid - . Wednesday would be suggested as a good day. On Thursday all of the newspapers would have the headline, "Raid at Grand Hotel, Gambling and Alcohol Discovered" and by Friday the hotel would be filled.

chapter 23

The Trolley Tour

After we had the Hotel History Tour up and running, my supervisor said she thought I should do a Trolley Tour.

"A what?" "How do you do that?"

Norris McPike, who had given trolley tours for hotel guests in the past, now gave area tours exclusively for guests of The Villas. My Supervisor suggested I go on one of his tours and she arranged for me ride along. Because his tours were for villa guests only there would not be a conflict with the hotel having a tour for our guests. I learned a lot about the local history from Norris.

First of all I learned that there had been a notorious gang of train robbers, The Reno Gang, from Seymour, Indiana that was responsible for doing the first train robbery in the United States. I never knew that. Another bit of local history I wasn't aware of was about a gang of robbers who lived in the hills surrounding the French Lick valley, not far from what is now the Pete Dye Golf Course. Norris even took the tour past the cemetery where some of the gang was buried. His tour was very well done and mostly it was pre-taped, allowing him to focus on his driving of the large van that carried his tour guests. I knew that I could never do a tour like his. For starters, I would **not** be driving the trolley, and his tour just wasn't my style. I wasn't sure what my style was but I knew, somehow, I would find it. So, with no sure plan in mind, I started giving trolley tours. I don't remember much about the first few tours except that Harold Morris was my first driver and he helped me a lot with the history.

When we started giving the trolley tours there was no sound system on board so I stood at the front of the trolley, holding on to two brass poles while trying to keep from falling as I shouted in order to be heard above the noise of the trolley. I pointed out the hotel's places of interest: the pro shop, golf courses, tennis courts, Pluto spring and stables. We would drive by the West Baden Springs Hotel building and I would encourage guests to take the Historic Landmarks tour.

As we drove through the town, there really wasn't much to see but I could look at downtown French Lick and my memory saw the businesses that had once been part of my French Lick.

Across the street from the plant I could still picture the Brown Building, that grand building that had once been the site of the most elegant casino that was considered to be second only to the casino at Monte Carlo. In the first floor of the Brown Building had been Miss Mohler's fine gift shop, the town's public works office and the Rexall Drug Store that also was the Greyhound Bus Terminal, all of them gone but still very much a part of my memories.

Moving across the street was the 'business district', where on one block of Maple Street was the center of French Lick. One would have found a department store called The Star Store. What I thought was the most wonderful feature of the Star Store was a thing the clerks put money in and *swoosh*, the gadget would take the money up through the ceiling and out of sight, just like magic. I remember the rabbit fur mittens that I fell in love with one Christmas Eve while we were doing some last minute shopping. Low-and-behold, Santa Claus must have read my mind because on Christmas morning those beautiful white and black fur mittens were under my Christmas tree. I also remember going with my mother one September day to The Star Store to buy my father a birthday present. I found the perfect gift, a beautiful doll whose eyes could open and close.

Daddy loved that doll so much that he let me take care of it for him. I didn't do a very good job. One day I was holding the doll and I was trying to figure out how her eyes could open and close and with my finger I pushed too hard on one of her eyes and pushed it all the way into her head. I was devastated.

Next to the Star Store was a men's clothing store and dry cleaners. There was a five and dime store, the movie theater, a bar, The Grand Hotel/restaurant, a hardware store, a dress shop, and a grocery store. This completed that side of the street.

The other side of the street on the corner of Maple and College Street was the corner drug store where high school kids used to gather afterschool and drink a coke and look at movie magazines. Berth's Little Dress Shop, another five and dime, a bowling alley and another small restaurant completed the businesses on that side. Next was the Wells Lot where band concerts took place in the summer and a large evergreen tree was lighted every Christmas. The cab company was also on the Wells Lot. All of this was on one little block in a town with less than 1,000 people.

Just north of the upper drug store was the bank. Our doctor's office was above the bank, so patients had to climb a long flight of stair to reach his office. If you made it up that flight of stairs, you were considered 'heart healthy'. Our dentist was just across the hall from the doctor. When he would be working on my teeth I fastened my gaze on his one glass eye.

The town had a furniture store, two funeral homes, a Ford dealership, a shoe factory, jewelry stores, post office, school, library; everything we needed was right in our own small town. Time had erased most of these establishments from French Lick but I could still see them, especially in the evening by the muted glow of the street lights.

Of course I couldn't tell our guest everything the town once offered - but I tried.

When I pointed out the little old building that had been our town's police station, my mind's eye still saw it at the foot of the hill behind the hotel with a light shining from within where the Chief of Police sat. He would have been in there alone because the building was only big enough for one man. In fact, that little building made the newspapers in Ripley's "Believe It Or Not", as the WORLD's SMALLEST POLICE STATION. About the same time, Ripley said that the Grand Hotel on Mackinac Island had the LONGEST PORCH IN THE WORLD at 880 feet. The porch is really 628 feet long, but as they say, "Never let the facts interfere with a good story."

On this tour we took the trolley past a free-standing smoke stack where the old tomato juice factory once stood. Tomato juice was 'invented' so to speak, at the French Lick Springs Hotel in 1917.

Tomatoes were at one time considered ornamental and even by some to be poisonous. My father referred to them as "love apples", and perhaps because of his original understanding of the fruit, would never eat a ripe, red tomato. He would, however, eat fried green ones.

When the factory was torn down the smoke stack refused to budge. They must have really known how to build a smoke stack back in the 1920's because it took an act of God to finally bring that smoke stack down. After surviving past its usefulness for several years, a bolt of lightning finally demolish that old smoke stack leaving us with just a memory of the Tomato Juice Canning Factory.

My first trolley driver was Harold Morris, a local area historian. He and all of my other drivers were far more informed about the history of the area than I and through them I learned a lot. One of them told me that the Police Chief would have to get a taxi to take a prisoner to the County Jail in Paoli because the Police Chief didn't have a car nor did he have a driver's license. No one ever explained to me how the prisoner was apprehended in the first place.

We drove past the Springs Valley School where Larry Bird, former player of the Boston Celtics, and Jerry Reynolds, former coach of the Sacramento Kings, had learned to play basketball. I explained how before 1957 French Lick and West Baden Springs had separate schools, small schools but big rivalries. Neither school had enough boys for a football team so, as in many small schools at that time in Indiana, basketball was "King".

However, in 1957-58 these two small schools consolidated into the Spring Valley School System. The French Lick "Red Devils", named for the Pluto water of French Lick and the West Baden "Sprudels", named for the Sprudel water of West Baden became the Springs Valley "Black Hawks".

The first school year, 1957-1958, of the Springs Valley Black Hawks, the boys' basketball team did something that this small valley had never expected. They were undefeated in their regular season and went all the way from the small gym at French Lick to play for the IHSAA championship in the Butler fieldhouse; there and only there did they lose their first game. They were defeated in the semi-final game by Fort Wayne South. This was back in the day when there was no "class" system in Indiana so small schools competed against large schools. When a small school's team made it to the final four that was big news and it didn't happen very often. Of course today schools are divided into divisions and play against schools of similar size.

The tour began to evolve; and even though the trolley's seats were hard and this was an open-air conveyance; windy and hot in summer and windy and cold in winter, we had a lot of fun.

Another one of my drivers was Oral Carnes, Jr., whom everyone calls "Junior", eventually provided me with a microphone so that I no longer had to hang-on for dear life and shout at the riders on the trolley. Junior also provided me with some one-liners that became part of the permanent (unwritten) script.

One day Junior pointed out the path across the Bendelow golf course where the Jersey and Holstein cattle were herded each morning to a pasture at the foot of Mt. Airie. I added that information to the tour and told that the dairy cattle provided milk, cream, buttermilk and butter to the hotel. Later, Junior told me in private that at night when the cattle were again taken back to the dairy barn, the herder would leave the gate to the pasture unlocked. It seems that quiet, secluded spot was a "lover's lane". So the next time we did a trolley tour as we were starting the ascent to Mt. Airie, I told the story about the pasture and its secret activity. After finishing the story I said, "Isn't that right, Junior?"

Junior fired back, "That's what the *big boys* told me." That got a big laugh. Suddenly, I had a flashback and said, "The *big girls* told me there were a lot of mosquitoes back there." That got another big laugh. Sometimes truth is funnier than fiction. This "routine" became a part of our permanent prater.

Junior wanted me to tell the story about the Archer Gang, a family who terrorized Orange and Martin counties in the 1880's, and lived in the hills near what is now the Pete Dye Golf Course. I kept trying to avoid the subject because what he wanted me to tell was that they had been lynched and that just didn't seem like something people would find entertaining. The former tour guide, Norris McPike, included the Archer gang story, even taking his van past the cemetery that is located across from the ninth hole of the Bendelow golf course where most of the Archer family is buried. I didn't like telling such a gruesome story but Junior always insisted. Finally, I decided it would be more palatable if I told it by way of a poem, sort of a chant. I called it "The Ballad of the Archer Gang". I would say a line and the guests would respond with 'The Outlaw Archer Gang'. I tried it out on a tour and it seemed to work better that way. On day a family was on the tour and the matriarch of the family said, "I think we should sing this." She started singing my poem to the tune of "Tom Dooley" and her family joined in. It was perfect. From then on we sang "The Outlaw Archer Gang" and everyone enjoyed the singing and learned the story but without dwelling on the gory details. We could laugh, not at the story but at ourselves.

Another driver, Jack Livingston, pulled a good one on me one time. We had just stopped so I could pass out copies of "The Outlaw Archer Gang". When I stood up and said that we were going to sing, the guests broke out laughing. I couldn't figure out what was so funny so I just smiled and proceeded to teach the song. After the tour was over and all the guests had left the trolley, Jack made a confession to me. While I was still in the lobby of the hotel before the tour, Jack told the guests who had boarded the trolley that, "The lady who does the tour is a nice lady but she does have a problem, she drinks. You can tell when she has been drinking because she always wants to sing." Thanks Jack.

I'm not sure which driver introduced me to Bear Cave but this became a very important part of our tour. We would drive past the location, stopping to point out the cave. Actually, the opening to the cave was only visible in late fall through early spring when there were no leaves on the trees to block the view so guests could rarely see the cave but we didn't let that stop us from telling this story:

"It seems that Jim Wilson, considered in his day to be a legendary hunter, came to the French Lick area around 1811 and decided to settle down in this place that was teeming with wild life. He built a cabin and planted a corn field.

"One morning Jim noticed that bear tracks led into his corn field and he was missing some ears of corn. This made Jim mad. He had worked too hard to share his corn with some old bear, so Jim set out, tracking the bear. Besides wanting to impose corporal punishment on the thief, bear meat was considered good eating and the skin was valuable for trading.

"Jim followed the bear tracks for several miles until he came to a cave. The bear tracks led into the cave. Some folks say that Jim made a lighted torch from sticks and such that he found outside the cave. So with the torch in one hand and his hunting rifle in the other hand, into the cave went Jim Wilson.

"Well, Jim found the bear and they engaged in hand-to-hand combat. The bear got scared and in his haste to get away from Jim, the bear accidentally brushed his paw over Jim's head and his claws scalped Jim Wilson. Jim came out of that cave bloody but not beaten and from that time on was known far and wide as 'Bear Jim Wilson'."

These and many other folksy tales made up our trolley tour, showing a side of French Lick that existed far, and I mean *really, really far,* from the glamour of the hotel.

In the summer of 2002, the West Baden Historical Society expressed an interest in going on a Trolley Tour. While the first time I had spoken to them I had been relaxed, telling about activities that we were doing at the hotel, I was somewhat nervous about this tour. Instead of showing the town to people for the first time I would be showing the town to people who probably knew more about the town than I did. Our granddaughter, Summer, had just graduated from college and was visiting us at that time. She and Johnny were the only people on that trolley who had less knowledge of the town's history than I, so I concentrated my tour on them; this helped me to not feel so intimidated. We were having so much fun and along the way we passed "Moonshine Holler" receiving that name for obvious reasons. Bob Lane, a lifelong resident of this valley started talking about his grandfather who was also a doctor and had delivered him; adding that this grandfather/doctor was also a bootlegger. I just handed Bob the mic and let him take over. His timing was perfect, his delivery droll and he had everybody in stitches. The next day I spoke to my supervisor and asked if we could hire Bob as a tour guide. She agreed and Bob became a very vital part of our history team. Bob was also a guide at the West Baden Hotel but I think he enjoyed the freedom he was given with the French Lick tours. Bob even created a Trolley Tour on the back roads to the Orangeville Amish community.

It was through Bob that Johnny and I learned about a house in French Lick that we could rent. It was just a hop, skip and a jump from the home where I had grown up.

Chapter 24

The House On Michigan Street

Our new home was on East Jackson Street. I never knew there was a West Jackson Street in French Lick until we had a medical emergency and the EMTs went to the wrong Jackson Street. They didn't know there was a West Jackson Street either until that day. GPS can certainly lead us into some unexpected places. Speaking of GPS, just for fun, my son Jeff and I let his GPS tell us how to go from French Lick to Bedford and what an adventure that was. It took us to back roads that I, having grown up in this area, had never seen. The route made travel so much more complicated than necessary. The only plus in following the GPS instructions and taking all those back roads is you won't experience much traffic; no locals would ever take that route.

This home was facing apartments where the former French Lick School had been, so every time I walked out my front door I was faced with the memory of my old schoolhouse that I had attended for twelve years. In fact, sometimes I would walk, circling the block, trying to retrace my steps as I remembered the many nights I would take the short cut onto the school grounds as I came home from church or the movies and feeling very close to the past. The sidewalks were the same but the hill had gotten steeper with the passing of the years.

154

In the back of our home was a street that had once been just an alley. I remember there being a log cabin that would have been on the back of what was now our back yard, facing the alley, and an old lady lived there. As a child I was fascinated with the outside of her home. I didn't know her name but she was one of my neighbors I had invited to my "June Party". As I recall, she accepted.

From this street I could see a sparsely wooded area that had once been my very own special woods. I could go there, all by myself, and sit on a big rock beside a tiny brook and think all sorts of wonderful thoughts. This magical place was right across from my home and Mother never had to worry about me. In fact, she could just look across the road a see me even though I was miles and miles away.

I could still see the trees that I watched on rainy afternoons from my front porch and imagined God was in the tops of those trees, and the place on a hill that I saw as I walked home from town where a tree formed a cross and became a distant shrine to me.

Sometimes when Johnny would be working late, playing the piano at Jack's Steakhouse in the hotel, I would walk down the street in front of my former home, remembering the many moonlit nights I walked there coming home from the movies or a basketball game.

I especially liked taking that walk in the winter when everything was covered with snow. I recalled the times when Daddy would let me go sledding down the hill, him on the sled and me giving him a big shove and then belly-flopping onto his back. He was a kid again.

Daddy always made me wear rubber gloves over my knitted gloves when I played in the snow to keep my hands dry.

To keep my feet dry, Daddy made me wear black boots that had these fasteners up the front, the kind farmers wore. They were very effective in keeping out the snow but not at all like the boots that other little girls wore. So I would just pretend I was wearing pretty girly galoshes with fur on top, and walk as lady-like as possible, trying to ignore the jingle of the metal clasps, while in reality looking like I just got in from milking the cows.

It was beginning to look like footwear would always be what "tripped me up", (pun intended) fashion wise; no cowboy boots, no pretty galoshes, and then, no white bucks.

When I arrived at the insecure early teen years and was needing to fit in, that is when white bucks became very popular. In case you don't know what white bucks are, they are not albino male deer. White Bucks are white suede oxford shoes made popular by Pat Boone, a singer/actor who was a teenage idol at that time. I was not what one might call a slave to fashion but I really wanted, really NEEDED a pair of white bucks. When at school, all I could see was a sea of white bucks covering the hall floors as students moved from one class to another; and sticking out, screaming, "Look at me, I'm different!" were my brown penny loafers. It got so bad that one Friday after school, I had to take to my bed in grief. To let you know just how serious this situation had become, this was Friday night during basketball season…need I say more? I just couldn't continue being the ONLY girl in school, in French Lick, perhaps the only girl in the WORLD who did not have a pair of white buck shoes.

But as I lay there, suffering in silence, or maybe not so silent, before game time a miracle happened. Aunt Betty appeared, just like a fairy godmother, and brought me a pair of WHITE BUCKS. And the moment I put them on my feet I was *healed*! I could now go the basketball game. Apparently my mother had interceded on my behalf and Aunt Betty had driven down to French Lick from Indianapolis with a brand new pair of white bucks. Now I would be just like the other girls, at least at school.

Looking at my childhood home in early 2000 was difficult. Yes, I could still imagine how it looked when I had lived there but it took a lot of imagining. The front porch had now been enclosed, and the entire home was covered with wood siding. The garages and my playhouse were all gone as were the trees I had loved so much. The Porter's home that had been next door was gone. Most of the other homes were still there so that helped a little. To add to the disconnect, the address had changed.

Now with my former home being almost unrecognizable, I had to rely on my memories of *432 Michigan Street*. Our basement was the full size of our house with a large room just inside the outside door that housed my father's work bench and tools. Hanging on the far wall of this room were a number of old muskets and powder horns that had been Great Aunt Julie's. My favorite feature of this room was the big work bench. Daddy had a large vice attached to the bench and I would use it to hold a piece of wood as I planed it. Why? I have no idea. I just liked to watch the shavings of wood curl up and fall to the floor. Daddy allowed me to putter around with his tools and I remember that at the tender age of 4 or 5 building a table. I used a somewhat square piece of wood and 4 long sticks of approximately the same length, and hammered one nail through the top of the table into the top of each leg. The legs had the unique quality of being able to spin.

There was another large room that had a big table in the middle where we put the potatoes and onions we had grown in our garden. Lining the walls were shelves holding quart jars of tomatoes, green beans, corn, peaches, blackberry and raspberry jelly, apple butter, and whatever else my mother had canned, all homemade.

My mother's wringer washing machine was in the room with our coal-burning furnace. Mother would carry all of the freshly laundered clothes upstairs and in warm weather, hang them on an outside line; in cold weather she dried our clothes on wooden racks placed over the floor heat registers.

Off of Daddy's workshop was a crawlspace where our cats liked to go to die. They would crawl way up to where no adult could reach them; so being the smallest person in the house I would crawl under the floor of the house while Daddy held a flashlight on the carcass; I'd grab the deceased cat by the tail and drag it out. A funeral would follow where I would officiate, with interment in the cat cemetery in our side yard, marked with small white crosses.

On the east side of the house was a porch that was shaded by the box elder tree, my climbing tree. I am 100% sure that if that tree were there today I could climb it. (Sorry for the visual.) In the winter the porch was glassed in and so cold that I would see where Jack Frost had been painting on the window panes. But in the summer, screens replaced the glass making it a perfect place to sleep.

During polio season, my half-sister, June, would bring her four boys to stay with us, taking them out of the city of Muncie, Indiana. Daddy put up a hammock on that porch and after all of us unsuccessfully protested to naps because of our advanced ages, we kids would scramble to grab the hammock, losers had to take the required afternoon nap on beds.

Daddy took advantage of the cool night air that sometimes made its way around the house and onto the porch and he put a roll-away bed out there for him to sleep on at night. Our chow-chow dog, Punky, who was an outside dog, would always sleep beneath the window where Daddy slept, the screened-in porch in summer and the front porch in the winter.

On the west side of the house, just outside of my bedroom window, was the place where I wore away all of the grass, practicing baton twirling.

~

When I was around ten years old life started to become more enjoyable. My mother ordered me a baton from the Montgomery Ward catalog. The circumference of that baton was about the size of a small tree. It came with a little how-to book with the catchy title, *How to Twirl*. I took the book and baton out to my back yard and started to teach myself baton twirling: how to do the side twirl, the horizontal, figure eight and other basic twirls. I got a lot of bumps and bruises as I tried to keep my arms and legs out of the way of the baton.

I took the baton to school so I could practice at recess and I think Mr. Alysworth, the band director, must have seen me because he encouraged me to take lessons from one of the majorettes, Marilyn Hill. I think he may have been trying to save me from seriously injuring myself.

In the summer when I was twelve, the majorette I had studied with could not march with the band in a parade because she was riding on a float, so Mr. Alysworth ask me to march in her place. Yippee! I could fit in her uniform but her boots were too small for me. We tried every shoe store in a thirty mile radius but no one had any majorette boots in stock and I needed them NOW. However, a man who worked at a store in Jasper had a daughter who had a pair that she no longer needed. We bought them and even though they were two sizes too big I wore them with extra socks throughout my high school marching band career. (Footwear again)

I was blessed to have some very good teachers including Nick Michaelaires. Nick twirled for the Marching One Hundred band at Indiana University. He and his wife, Joyce, operated a baton and dance studio in Bloomington, Indiana, so I eventually got to take both dance and baton lessons from him. One dance he was teaching me required a shimmy of the shoulders......I refused to do *that*. Just imagine how I would have reacted to the dance moves of today.

For the first time in my life I was doing something I wanted to do. I would practice twirling in the side yard of our home from breakfast until supper in the summer and in the gym when it was available on school days. In the winter on Saturdays I would practice in the power plant. The second engine room at the plant had a high shaft in the middle with a skylight and I could practice my high throws in there.

I liked the medals and trophies I won because they affirmed that I was achieving my goals but they were not the main reason I twirled. I just LIKED the physical activity, the combination of dance and athletics.

I still had to practice the piano, ugh, but at least I was enjoying *one* of my disciplines.

Chapter 25

This Is Where We Came In

Perhaps the lowest point for the hotel came when the French Lick Hotel was put up for auction in 1991. Some potential buyers were even considering demolishing the buildings and calculating how many bricks they would yield.

But thankfully, Luther James of Louisville, Kentucky, bought the hotel just minutes after the auction was opened for $2.6 million.

Mr. James wanted to return the hotel to its former appearance, before Sheraton's modernization. Perhaps the most significant improvement that Luther James made to the hotel was to remove the black and white tiles from the lobby floor, exposing the beautiful mosaic tiles from the Taggart years.

Another ownership change came when Boykin Lodging of Cleveland Ohio, made Luther James 'an offer he couldn't refuse', approximately $20 million in 1997, and, as they say, "…that is where we came in".

When we arrived in French Lick in January 2000, the guest count during the week was usually quite low with whole wings standing empty. On Friday evenings in January and February we had a lot of skiers check-in for Paoli Peaks but on Sunday they would check-out, leaving the hotel once more with a lot of empty rooms.

One night after a Blue and Gold banquet I took the Cup Scouts on a tour of the Presidential Suite. I left the lights on in the suite when we finished the tour and I had to go back later and turn them off. As I walked down the long, deserted hall I said, out loud, "Okay, IF there are any ghosts around here, NOW would be a good time to show yourselves." I was met with silence. I am happy, or sorry, depending on your point of view, to report that not one whiff of cold air, nor movement of curtains, nor eerie sound did I encounter.

After the spring rains started in late February/early March and washed away the snow on the Peaks, our clientele began to change as we welcomed various convention groups along with our many faithful guests who returned to the hotel on a regular bases.

I noticed that there were basically two important reasons that guests returned to our hotel; the first, and perhaps the most important, was the way our staff made them feel welcome with that good old Hoosier Hospitality. Many guests have formed very close friendships with our staff, even sending hand knitted blankets to new babies or someone recovering from surgery. One very special couple came to the hotel several times each year and we always anticipated their visits just as one does when expecting to see a member of one's family. They always came for New Year's Eve but rather that joining the festivities in the Ball Room they chose to celebrate in the bowling alley bar with one of our staff who had become a very good friend. This same couple even returned to French Lick to attend the funeral of one of our staff, being a part of good times and bad.

The second reason guests returned was because of the history surrounding this hotel. A couple who had gone on my tour came back the following year with their entire wedding party and guests. They said they loved the history of the hotel and that they wanted to be a part of that history. They chose to be married in our garden and asked Johnny to play the accordion for the ceremony. I well remember that day because it was on our daughter's birthday, July 21st, and I think it was the hottest, most humid day of that entire summer.

On an early fall day, two tour coaches arrived from the Piggott State Bank of Piggott, Arkansas, with 83 guests on board. I was especially delighted to meet one of the members of the tour named Josephine, age 97. Josephine made this long trip because she wanted to see the place where her parents had spent their honeymoon.

The Real Scoop on Celebrities

I know it isn't fair to expect someone in the public eye to always be who they portray on screen or when running for a public office but there is no excuse for not being kind. I heard from staff members about a certain TV actor who was drunk and disorderly during his entire stay at the hotel. I heard about an angelic faced singer who was rude and demanding, and about a very wealthy restaurant chain developer who never said "thank you" or gave anyone a tip.

But one celebrity couple who did NOT disappoint were Ronald and Nancy Reagan.

Just as her mother and sisters had been telephone operators at the hotel, my mother had also worked at the big switchboard during the Sheraton years. Late one night in November 1971, after mother got home from work, she called me and said, "I just saw Ronnie and Nancy dancing in the lobby." That was when the Republican Governors were meeting at the French Lick Sheraton Hotel. She also said, "Everyone is saying to keep an eye on Reagan, he will be President someday." How right they were.

The Reagans made quite an impact on many of the hotel's staff but perhaps none so much as on Don Anderson.

When I met Don Anderson in 2000, he was working as a bellman at the hotel. Don had once been a member of the security staff but with a new owner came a new requirement-all security personnel had to have a driver's license. Don didn't have a driver's license; he had never learned to drive.

Don lived just a couple of blocks from the hotel and he walked to work. His first job had been at the hotel and he had never worked anywhere else.

Don had this great talent for describing food that was in the employees' dining room. He usually took the early lunch hour and then came back and told the other bellmen and me what was being served. He could make our mouths' water as he described the wonderful food he had just eaten. When we went to the dining room we would stand, staring at the buffet, wondering, "Where did Don eat?" His delicious prime rib was just dried up, overdone, curled up, something that resembled beef jerky; the buttery mashed potatoes were watery, instant from a box and the vegetable unrecognizable; but to Don he had just had a feast.

One cold December night hardly anyone was in the hotel but a front desk clerk, dining staff, Don Anderson and me. We were waiting for a tour bus to arrive from Illinois.

Refreshments had been prepared for their arrival and I was to greet the group. Don was the only bellman on duty.

The bus was over an hour late due to the mix-up with time zones, Illinois being on central time and our area in Indiana being on eastern time. It was also snowing so that compounded the problem. Every once in a while Don would go to the lower entrance and shovel snow off the walk leading down to the front of the hotel. Then he would come back up to the lobby to get warm, sometimes standing in front of my desk, talking to me about when he had been a security guard and had to shoo teenager, Tommie McDonald, my little brother, off the property; or about how some employees were not allowed to work when the Indiana Supreme Court Judges were at the hotel because of prior convictions (employees' convictions not the Judges').

His favorite story was about when the Reagans were at the hotel in 1971, and that he had been assigned to their security team. He told me that Vice President Agnew was given the Governors Suite and the Presidential Suite was reserved for President Nixon who never arrived. According to Don, the Reagans were on the seventh floor because that was the most secure area.

Don said that when the Reagans were leaving they invited him to visit them on their ranch as a thank you for the excellent way he had taken care of them while at the hotel.

Between stories he would go look out the front door to see if there was any sign of our tour group.

Finally I heard him say, "Eva Sharron, Here's your bus." He turned and went down the inside stairs to take the luggage cart out and start bringing in the luggage. I went down the front steps to the bus to meet and greet the guests and escort them up to the hotel.

While they were enjoying the refreshments I noticed that Don hadn't yet brought up any luggage so I went down to see what the holdup was. At the bottom of the stairs I saw Don lying on his back with one leg bent, knee up, and as silly as it may sound my first thought was, "Why is Don sleeping on the floor?"

But reality quickly set in and when he didn't respond to me I went to the phone booth that was just a couple of steps away from Don to call for help. The phone had been removed! So I ran upstairs and told the desk clerk to call 911 and security, that Don was unconscious, and then I turned around and ran back down stairs. The two women who were the tour guides for the bus group were already performing CPR on Don. They had heard me asking for help and had sprung into action. They worked on him until the rescue squad arrived. At that point I'm not sure who arrived next except I know that the hotel security guard and the coroner were there and after a time it was declared that Don was gone. I don't know who had called Johnny but I was aware that he was by my side during this time comforting me and praying.

After Don was taken away, Johnny and I went upstairs to the lobby where all of the people from the bus tour were still sitting, silently waiting for any news. I had to tell them that Don had passed away and I thanked the ladies who had been so quick to respond to this emergency. All of the people from the tour, of their own accord, joined hands, reaching out to include Johnny and me and formed a circle there in the lobby. Amid tears from these kindhearted people, someone in the group said a most beautiful prayer for Don and his family.

The next morning the group was scheduled to have a tour of the hotel. One of the guides of the group offered to cancel the tour; they thought I might find it too hard to lead them through the hotel, particularly where I had found Don the night before. I thanked them for their consideration but I knew Don would have wanted me to do the tour. It was the most difficult tour I ever gave but I did it to honor Don Anderson.

Chapter 26

Remnants Of The Past

In some ways, Thomas Wolfe was right when he said, "You Can't Go Home Again", but Johnny and I were blessed to be able to "Go Home Again", at least for a little while. French Lick had been our first home together. When we returned, things had not changed all that much but what had changed had not been for the better.

Many buildings were still standing; some with different functions but nevertheless they were still there; and some represented only by an empty lot to remind us of what had been.

When the public television station WFYI was preparing to do a segment about the restoration of the hotel on the show *ACROSS INDIANA*, the hotel asked me to be the spokesperson. As the television crew was setting up for the taping of the show, the interviewer asked me how long I had worked at the hotel. One thing led to another and she became interested in my family. A member of the crew asked if I had any pictures of when Johnny and I met. I had to admit we didn't have very many, just our wedding pictures. They asked if Johnny could bring what we did have. I called Johnny and he grabbed what he could find and hurried over with the pictures. As the interview was progressing the photographer wanted Johnny to be in the show. When we finished with the taping Johnny and I didn't give any more thought to the show. We knew from past experience that very little of interviews were actually aired.

A few weeks later on a Saturday night I got a call from Elsie Thurston. Elsie was the mother of one of my friends at French Lick High School and she had also been the school's secretary back when I was in school. Elsie said she had just seen me on television and the show made her homesick. I asked her where she lived and she said, "In French Lick." She was homesick for the French Lick of the past.

Johnny and I didn't have television service or a computer at that time (our choice) and we had to go to the library to see the show. We were so surprised to see the title for that episode, #1710, was "Through One Woman's Eyes" and to see both of us appearing in the show.

One thing that did not go away or even charge was the *sound* of French Lick. The voice-that southern Indiana accent and the expressions people use-would bring a smile to my face. But there was one expression I didn't remember and it baffled me. I was often greeted with, "You okay?" or "You alright?" I began to worry. Finally I asked Johnny if I looked sick or tired. He said, "No. Why?" I told him people kept asking me if I was 'Okay?' Johnny explained that that was their way of saying, "How are you?" He picked-up on that way before I did.

And the sound of thunder. Living so many years in the flat land of northwestern Ohio, I had grown use to the sound of thunder crashing and they being gone. But in the valley of French Lick and West Baden the thunder BOOMS and BOOMS and BOOMS again and again as the hills toss the sound to one another until they get tired of the game called "echo" and let the sound roll silently down into the valley.

Perhaps the most poignant reminders of days gone by were the smells; the smell of Pluto water and the smell of coal dust. It had been many years since the last coal car had come down the railroad tracks that ran between the power plant and the building next to the highway. Coal had been the fuel for the hotel for many years. My father said that on one very cold day alone the hotel had burned 50 tons of coal. In the late 40's they were burning 30 tons a day.

Only a remnant of the railroad tracks could be seen on the hotel property but what I could see brought back memories of coal cars clanging to a stop beside the power house.

The place where I had written my "E-VA" in the wet cement when I was five years old, joining the V to the A to save time, was gone, but I could still mark the spot.

However to my surprise and delight, I could still smell the coal dust. I took every opportunity to walk beside the power plant, just to take a deep breath and remember the time of my father's life at the power plant.

Chapter 21

Orange Shirts

After our visit to the French Lick hotel in 1998, we were so zoned in on moving back to French Lick that we were completely ignorant of the gambling issue that was swirling around, threatening to disturb the peace of the valley for some, while stirring up the possibility of prosperity for others.

While the state of Indiana had an unemployment rate of 5.2 %, Orange County's unemployment rate was running at 9% and sometimes even higher. The one thing everyone in the county could agree on was that *something* needed to be done to offer employment to the valley.

The eleventh casino license in Indiana had been issued to Patoka Lake, but because the Army Corps of Engineers owned the reservoir the license would never be used.

In all of our forty-plus years together, gambling, or to be more specific, casinos, had never entered either of our minds….we didn't even buy lottery tickets. But now we found ourselves in the epicenter of the controversy: should there be a casino in the French Lick/West Baden valley?

In 2000 the hotel asked me to be interviewed by a reporter from the Louisville *Courier-Journal* newspaper about the history of the hotel. She asked me who were some famous people who had stayed at the hotel and if I had ever met any of them. I named a few I had heard of visiting: Bing

Crosby, Bob Hope, Lana Turner, Howard Hughes, Franklin and Eleanor Roosevelt, Joe and Rose Kennedy,...then I suddenly remembered when I had met Harry S Truman.

One of the biggest thrills in my life surrounding the hotel was when the Indiana Democratic Editors Convention held their annual meeting in August of 1955. President Harry S Truman had attended the convention and our high school band welcomed him by playing what else but "The Missouri Waltz". I was the Drum Majorette and was directing the band. As we were playing, Mr. Alysworth, our band director, told me to hand the baton to Mr. Truman, so he could lead our band. Mr. Truman didn't take the baton but took my hand instead. Just at that moment, a newspaper photographer took our picture but I didn't know which newspaper.

The next day, her article appeared in her paper and there was my picture with Mr. Truman, taken nearly 50 years before. She had found it in her paper's archives.

This was the first interview I had ever done and when she asked me, "How do you feel about a casino being built here?", I was caught off guard. I had in mind what Branson, Missouri had done to revitalize their town, so I answered that I would like to see additional options pursued to revitalize Orange County, "not putting all our eggs in one basket". When the article was printed, a manager came to my desk and said, "You better hope that the owners of the hotel don't read that article." He was implying that I could lose my job. (Like my opinion was going to sway the gaming commission one way or the other.) Looks like they didn't read the article.

A large constituency of folks from Orange County banded together, proudly wearing orange shirts and appeared at the Indiana Statehouse on a regular basis to remind the legislators that Orange County wanted and needed a casino. It worked.

In 2003, the bill was passed and signed by Governor Frank O'Bannon that moved the casino license from Patoka Lake to Orange County. Now someone was needed to actually build the casino.

Rumors ran rampant during this period of uncertainty. Local folks were trying to guess where the casino should be built, and everyone had an opinion. Indiana law stated that any casino built in Indiana had to be on water. Some of us thought that with the valley's propensity for flooding, that would not be a problem. Our little Lick Creek (properly pronounced *Crick* and rhymes with *Lick*) that ran through the valley certainly wasn't big enough to float much more that an inner tube. Of course, our annual January and May floods could float rowboats and canoes but the water always subsided within a few days.

There were a lot of problems to overcome but these didn't dampen the enthusiasm of the prospect of prosperity for the valley.

Since I had never seen a casino, at least not one I recognized to be a casino, I did not have an opinion one way or the other as to a probable location. The need for it to float did mystify me a little. Then when the laws changed to simply require a casino to have "a water feature" I was further confused. How was water and gaming connected? Maybe the next law would require people to stand in a puddle of water while buying a lottery tickets.

While my interest in the casino was scant, my interest in the hotel was huge. Like most of the hotel staff, I didn't want the beauty and historical charm of *our* hotel to be compromised by the casino.

When Donald Trump was granted Indiana's 11th casino license in 2004, Boykin Lodging, of Cleveland was the owner of the hotel. The hotel was in need of much more than T L C; it was in such poor condition that our General Manager once told me to direct our guests to activities OUTSIDE the hotel as much as possible. Faithful guests returned year after year, in spite of the condition of the hotel, because of the hospitality of our employees. We wanted to see the hotel receive the many repairs that were desperately needed.

But by the end of the year, Trump Hotel and Casino Resorts had filed for bankruptcy. By May, the state tax court found that the Trump group owed $18 million in back taxes. Trump Hotel and Casino Resorts decided to not use the gaming license. The Governor of Indiana, Mitch Daniels, had called for the resignation of the state Gaming Commission that had awarded the license to Trump, so the new members of the Indiana Gaming Commission began searching for a more financially stable source to build the French Lick Casino.

Sometimes at the end of my Hotel History Tour during the question and answer time, guests would ask about the possible future of the hotel. I would honestly say that I had no inside information on what was happening with the casino nor the hotel. But I always said that I was confident that this hotel would always be here. One day a guest said, "This hotel will one day be owned by a family much like the Taggarts", just as if she knew.

I responded, "Oh, I hope so.", but I really didn't see how that could happen.

Chapter 28

Happy Days Really Are Here Again!

On a mid-April morning in 2005, I could actually feel a difference in the atmosphere as I walked into the hotel. There were a lot of people in the lobby considering it was a weekday. When I arrived at my desk I noticed a change in the faces of the staff. They had always been cordial; putting on their "game faces", but now they were actually smiling real smiles that showed in their eyes. Right away, the bell captain, Sam Townsley, approached my desk and whispered, "Mr. Cook bought the hotel." I made him repeat it, "Mr. Cook bought the hotel."

"*OUR* Hotel?"

"Yes, *OUR* Hotel"

Now I understood. All of the staff must be thinking what first came into my mind, "Now the hotel will be brought back to the way it should be." We had seen what had been done at West Baden and we trusted Mr. Cook to do right by us.

One by one my good buddies at the bell stand drifted over to me, making positive comments about our future. One of the bellman, said, "There is Mr. Cook over by those guys.", indicating a group of men dressed in khaki pants and button-down shirts, looking and pointing at the ceiling of the lobby. I had never seen Mr. Cook so I asked which one was he. "He's the one everyone else is looking at." And that was the only way I could distinguish him from the others. From that day on I never saw Bill Cook dressed in anything but khaki pants and a long-sleeved, button-down shirt, except on the occasions of two Christmas parties for the staff and his son's wedding.

Later that week, Mr. Cook came to my desk and introduced himself to me. He called me E(long e) va and I corrected him, explaining for whom I was named and the tradition of the short e. He never forgot.

There were also a lot of new faces, men and women wearing business suits, and we soon learned that they belonged to Benchmark Hospitality Management.

Mr. Cook had hired Benchmark Management Company to manage the West Baden Springs Hotel, or so they thought. But to their surprise when he was meeting with them and looking at a mock-up of the two hotels, Mr. Cook said he wanted them to manage "this hotel" and pointed to the French Lick Hotel building. He knew that the success of the French Lick Springs Hotel and the casino were paramount to the success of the West Baden Hotel.

When Bill Cook entered the picture and started the ball rolling to re-do the French Lick Hotel, more than just the landscape began to change. He knew that for the West Baden Hotel to survive the French Lick Hotel had to be in top form and, like the majority of people, when asked, would have agreed, the casino was a necessity.

Changes began immediately. Tarps were laid, furniture moved or removed. My desk was in a constant state of flux.

Originally my desk was positioned in the middle of the lobby, between two pillars, facing the front entrance. One day a worker dressed in a hazmat suite set up his ladder in front of my desk and proceeded to climb the ladder and poke and prod the ceiling above and to the right of my head.

I began to wonder why he needed that suit and I didn't? I decided that was a good time for me to leave my desk and stand at the bellmen's desk.

Soon I was moved closer to the hall leading to the garden wing. During this time our entire hotel welcomed a convention of Mastiff dog owners and their dogs. My desk had been moved to a place in the lobby that was in line with the path that a certain Mastiff walked each day. I'm thinking he must have liked me a lot because he 'marked' my desk every time he passed it.

The original plan was to close one wing at a time and re-do that wing, then move to another wing and so on and so forth. This way guests could still come to the hotel and the staff would not lose their employment.

When the first wing was closed employees were given the opportunity to choose furniture, TVs, pictures, glassware, and all sorts of things that were being discarded. I brought home some pictures, a table, and other odd and ends. At that point, Johnny said that we had enough stuff and not to bring anything else home. Well, I saw the glass stemware that was still up for grabs and decided that we really could use twenty of those glasses for our family's Thanksgiving Dinner that we would be hosting. The security guard, Gwen, came up with a solution and we entered into a conspiracy. She stored the twenty glasses in a box in the security office and every night when I went home from work I took two of the glasses, hid them in my briefcase, and spirited them home, hiding them in a little-used cabinet in our kitchen.

One night there was a real police officer guarding the back entrance to the hotel. When I started to leave for home Gwen handed me my two glasses and I hid them in my briefcase as usual. Then we noticed the officer watching us with a suspicious eye. We just stood our ground, returning look for look. Then he said, "I'm not even going to ask."

The week before Thanksgiving Johnny said we needed to buy some glasses for the dinner. I took him to the kitchen and with a "Ta Da!" flung open the cabinet door and proudly showed him the beautiful glass stemware. The look of surprise on his face was priceless.

~

The front wing facing east was the first to be closed and work began in earnest on the floors above the small gift shop, the ladies clothing shop, Jack's Steakhouse and various offices. One day a crow bar came falling through the ceiling of the small gift shop and impaled its self in the floor where the salesperson had just been standing.

While that wing was closed we had a group of middle-school kids come to the hotel for a church convention. The only thing those kids needed was to see a sign that read CLOSED and getting onto that wing became the main reason for their being at the hotel. They kept Security hopping during their entire stay.

By the first of November it had become apparent that keeping the hotel open was proving to be too dangerous for both guests and staff. Also, the work was moving more slowly than had been anticipated.

The week before Thanksgiving, the entire staff was called to a meeting where we were informed that the hotel would be closed immediately. A noticeable hush fell over the room and I got a sinking feeling in my stomach, the hotel closed! I was sure everyone was thinking what I was thinking, "We would all be out of work." But then we were told that we would all get unemployment and we should not feel badly about that because we had all paid into it. Also, since unemployment benefits were only a portion of our usual income, *the company would issue us checks every two weeks making up the difference*, and we would to be able to sign up at the hotel; Work One would come to us.

As we were all trying to absorb this great news, we were next told that those of us who had medical insurance through work would be eligible for COBRA but because the cost for that is prohibitive to most of us, we would only pay what we normally paid and *the company would pay the difference for us*. What we were hearing was generosity beyond imagination.

At that point, Mr. Cook, who was sitting in front of me, turned around and said, "Eva, do you think they will all stay?"

I was so choked up I could barely answer, "Yes, I'm sure they will." It was very important to him that the current employees would remain as part of the new French Lick Springs Hotel.

And stay we did. There was a lot of work for us to do before the hotel could be completely turned over to the construction or the more fitting name, destruction, crew.

All of the furniture, pictures, glassware, pots and pans, etc. were either given to the employees, given to charities or sold to the general public.

I was part of the team that was packing up all of the treasures that would be taken to Bloomington for safe keeping: pictures of the Kentucky Derby winners, antique dishes, plaques and all sorts of memorabilia. Every day as staff would uncover another object of interest they would bring it to our workroom on the fifth floor and we would pack it up with the rest of the things going to Bloomington. For the first few days we would ride the elevator up and down, to and from our workroom but it wasn't long before the elevators were disabled and we had to walk the five flights of marble stairs. We had to pack our lunch but could still eat in the employees dining area. We wore hard hats and masks in the lobby area. Every time we came out of our workroom there was less of the hotel and more of what just looked like ruins. When the water was turned off we women on the fifth floor had to get creative with the bathroom facilities. We found that the bathroom in each guest room was good for one last flush, so we would just find a different guest room and finished it off.

The cold December day when I looked out the window from the fifth floor and saw them bringing in a long line of blue and pink port-a-potties, I decided it was time for me to leave.

Through all of this Mr. Cook could be seen driving his pick-up truck, hauling stuff here and there, laughing, smiling, calling greetings, thoroughly enjoying every minute of this vast project. I thought about

Tom Taggart, the man who would have been found in the midst of the planning and construction of what was now being restored after 100 years.

To think that a woman had predicted this and it was now true. How could she have known?

The last time for all of the pre-renovation employees, approximately 300 of us, to be together was an emotional time. We had all grown very close as we prepared for a future that would be so wonderful for our beloved hotel. But we knew that with the beginning of this new era, we would never again enjoy the closeness we had felt through the difficult years. A new history was being written.

~

The months when the hotel was closed were not idle times. Between the closing of the hotel and its reopening, Mr. Cook, with the assistance of Ivy Tech, provided the opportunity for all of the employees to improve our computer skills, reading abilities, hospitality skills, and many other areas where we wanted improvement. Some of our employees even earned their GEDs.

Employees were also assigned to different jobs that were needed to help expedite this massive project.

It was exciting and disconcerting all at the same time as the entire valley was alive with charge. The changes to the hotel were only part of what was happening.

It seemed as if every street and sidewalk in French Lick was torn up, and all at the same time. I generally walked to and from work and with no sidewalks I fell twice due to the debris that covered the streets, even having to go to the ER on one occasion. The only plus for me was when my face hit the street in front of the hotel and I saw the original bricks that had made up the first street.

The hill behind the hotel was getting smaller as bulldozers and other earth movers grabbed huge scoops to earth, loading dump trucks that carried tons of earth to the grounds around the hotel; the top of Mt. Airie was being turned in the Pete Dye Golf Course; the stables were being moved from Mt. Airie to the West Baden Hotel property; a new convention center was going up with a parking garage, and all of this happening because of a casino.

The casino was being constructed to look like a boat, complete with a waterwheel on one side, a wheelhouse on top and a "water feature" around it.

Well, I had wished I could have seen French Lick through my father's eyes in the early 1900's and I was getting my wish. This must have been what it was like one hundred years ago when both hotels were alive with change. Our air was saturated with dirt and dust, and traffic was so congested that it could take half an hour to drive a quarter of a mile from the hotel to Dairy Queen. Of course there was no Dairy Queen in my father's day nor would there have been cars on the road, but trying to drive a wagon with horses must have been even more difficult. This taught me that "the good ole' days" may have not been as wonderful as I had thought. I also learned to be more careful what I wished for, I just might get it.

I am not thrilled with change. But for me, the saddest change came the day that the smoke stack, the only thing that still remained of the power plant, was destroyed.

That smoke stack didn't go down without a fight. I was standing next to Mr. Cook who kept telling it to, "Fall, fall." and finally he was shouting, "Down! Down!" And it came down.

At that same moment down came my tears when the last remnant of my father's sixty year work-life was reduced to rubble…and I could no longer smell the coal dust.

While my heart was sad to see this part of the hotel taken down, my head knew that this was necessary. The hotel had been the very reason there was a town at all and the hotel would be the reason for the town to survive. Like it or not, life is full of beginnings and endings, and I don't like endings. However, all I could do was accept and adjust. I am sure that my father would have accepted the new beginning even as he would have regretted seeing the old power plant crumble.

~

Later in the summer I was asked to attend a meeting at the West Baden Springs Hotel where I was informed that all tours, which included the French Lick History Tour and Trolley Tour, would now be given by Historic Landmarks tour guides. Historic Landmarks had been very instrumental in the saving of the West Baden Springs Hotel building and the additional tours would provide more income for the foundation.

This change hit me the hardest personally. Developing the Hotel History Tour and the Trolley Tour had been something new for me and had forced me to move in unfamiliar territory. I had learned so much and grown in ways I had never expected. Besides learning more about both the hotel's and town's history, I learned a lot about myself. One thing I learned was that I enjoyed speaking to large groups of people. The highlight of my day was giving a tour or speaking to a convention group about the hotel. But now it looked as if all of that was in the past. Once again I had to choose what I would do next; would I wallow in lose or look for new possibilities. I chose to look for new possibilities.

The new possibility took me in the direction of the Human Resource Department.

Chapter 29

New Challenges

When I joined the Human Resource Department in the summer of 2006, we were in the process of hiring approximately 1,100 new employees before the hotel and casino opened in November. We had job applications to consider, references to check, and tons of paperwork. This was all right down my alley; I liked checking references and, call me weird but, I love paperwork: filing, organizing, handling papers. I was also working in an office with a great group of wonderful, and sometimes wacky, people who made my new job a joy.

As the hiring process moved along we were presented with the challenge of orientation for all of the new employees. Besides all of the usual forms to explain and sign, we had classes to help the new hires understand their own personality types and how everyone was vital to the hotel.

Sometimes I shared my story of taking a job in a nursing home that I was not thrilled with but by looking for opportunities to move into a better position finally achieving a job I really loved. I had learned that any job can be a stepping stone or a stumbling block, it's up to us what we make of it.

I would even share with them about being hired as the concierge and then having to look up *'concierge'* in a dictionary to see what I had been hired to do. Sometimes we just need to take a chance. When Johnny and I were working for ourselves at KOBEE'S PIANO SERVICE, we had a saying pinned to a bulletin board that read, "You can't reach second base and keep your foot one first." How true.

Another part of orientation was to acquaint the new employees with the history of the hotel and that became my main job. My love for the hotel and its history had grown to the point that I wanted to tell every guest about it, but of course that would be impossible. But now I had the opportunity to do just that by sending out well-informed employees to accomplish my mission. I stressed to the employees how guests were not always going to wait until they could find a hotel historian to answer questions and would very likely ask whomever of the staff was near them. I learned how to put together a power point for my presentation and emphasized the importance for them to know the right answers.

Eventually, I accepted the challenge to plan and carry out tours for all of the employees so that everyone could know everything that was available at the resort. They visited both hotels, all restaurants, both spas, both pools, the stables, the three golf courses and pro shops, and the casino. Being given special permission to show non-casino staff the casino was very special because in Indiana, if you work for a property with a casino, you are not allowed in that casino except to work. Most of our employees fell in that category, including me.

My goal was to show every employee all that the resort had to offer. That way every employee could better appreciate the entire resort, recommend activities, give directions, and just maybe see the next stepping stone for their own future.

A change of venue was in store for Johnny also.

With the reopening of the French Lick Springs Hotel in November, 2006, there was no longer anyplace for Johnny to play the piano at the French Lick hotel.

The lobby's piano was gone. Jack's steakhouse was gone. The large dining room was gone. In all of this big, beautiful, spectacular hotel there was no place for a piano. Johnny's dream was beginning to fade.

But prior to the grand opening at the West Baden Springs Hotel, that hotel's manager asked Johnny to play the concert grand piano in the atrium when they opened in May of 2007. This was absolutely the best news that could come to Johnny. His dream that looked as if it were dimming had just been waiting until the right moment for God to bring it to light.

As I sat in the atrium the night of the opening listening to Johnny's beautiful piano music fill the atrium, the sunlight began to fade and the changing lights at the top of the dome became visible. Then I noticed the lights from the guest rooms begin to come on, one by one, and I felt as if I were watching the opening of the West Baden Springs Hotel in 1902.

I more fully understood what this valley was all about and I understood what Lee Sinclair had brought to the West Baden Hotel. There was a serenity one felt when entering this vast atrium. This calming spirit and the beautiful music continued to gently place a benediction over me every night as I sat in the atrium while Johnny played the piano. It was a confirmation to the human need to cease from work and to rest.

The first time he heard Johnny play at the West Baden Springs Hotel, Mr. Cook came over, lifted the piano lid to its full height and put up the prop stick. He said that he wanted everyone to hear Johnny's music.

Johnny continued to play the piano regularly at West Baden on weekends and was featured as the pianist for the cocktail hour in the atrium on New Year's Eve 2008. After the cocktail hour a big band played during the dinner and for dancing so we were able to leave West Baden shortly after Johnny finished playing the piano that night. On the way home I suggested that we stop at the French Lick Hotel. Guests were already in the ballrooms enjoying the New Year's Eve activities leaving the hotel's lobby surprisingly silent. We quietly walked through the hotel, holding hands, each absorbed in our own thoughts.

My first thought was how wonderful it was to have this handsome man whom I had first met right here in this very hotel lobby so many years before now walking beside me.

It may sound corny but to be in the place where my parents had walked and worked gave me such a feeling of still being a part of them. Perhaps the French Lick Springs Hotel is the one thing that has been a constant part of my life; a place that is still there from my youth. My school I attended has been torn down, my church has been torn down, my home looks nothing like it did when I was growing up, but the hotel, *my* hotel, is still standing and now thriving. To me, the French Lick Springs Hotel is so much more than just a place to work, it actually has a feeling of a place to belong.

After leaving the lobby we stepped outside to enjoy the beautiful Christmas lights in the garden and then went home to greet 2009 with our usual quiet celebration.

Chapter 30

Bittersweet

Johnny and I were married on October 3, 1958, on a Friday night. Our honeymoon lasted but the week-end and I returned to Bloomington on Monday to resume my studies at Indiana University. On Wednesday, Johnny came to visit me and we went to Brown County State Park and had lunch in Nashville, Indiana at a charming little restaurant. On our way back to IU we stopped at a roadside produce farm where a lady was selling smalls bundles of bittersweet. I loved the fall colors that were captured in these plants and Johnny bought a bouquet for me.

Fifty years later, on October 3, 2008, we celebrated our Golden Wedding Anniversary by renewing our vows at our church. I wanted to use the Order for Marriage from the *Service Book and Hymnal* that was in use fifty years before. Our young pastor had some difficulty with the King James language used in the old hymnal but he came through and had us "*take thee*" and "*thereto I plight thee my troth,*". Perhaps the most touching time during the service for me was when Johnny and I served Holy Communion to our family. As each precious one stepped up to receive the Bread and the Wine, my heart was overflowing with emotion and I silently offered a prayer of thanksgiving for the blessing of each and every member of our family.

Our first New Year's Eve together was Wednesday, December 31, 1958, and Johnny had been playing with the Ted Huston Orchestra at the French Lick Sheraton Hotel. On Wednesday, December 31, 2008, 50 years later, he was playing the piano at the West Baden Springs Hotel's New Year's Eve Gala. That turned out to be the last New Year's Eve party where Johnny would play. Three weeks later Johnny suffered a stroke that ended his professional career.

A second, more severe stroke occurred on December 27, 2011, and life for us went from staying in hospitals, to home-health care, to nursing homes, and finally to hospice. I thank God for being able to stay near my husband and being blessed with taking care of him, becoming his full-time nurse during most of the last four years as we grew closer to each other and to God.

We were blessed that Johnny, through all of his losses, was still able to speak and express his thoughts and feelings, tell jokes, and, most importantly, he could say, "I love you", often adding, "forever and beyond". He said that every day and many times each day, never wanting his family to forget. And he told us right up to the very end.

Johnny passed from his suffering on December 18, 2015, and was laid to rest on December 22, 2015, his 80th birthday. We all sang "Happy Birthday" at the service in celebration of his first heavenly birthday.

I know without a doubt that he is totally healed and in the presence of our Lord and Savior, Jesus Christ.

Postscript

The French Lick Springs Hotel has been welcoming guests for over 160 years, through good times and not so good times. It has a special spirit that has been felt by the faithful employees who have kept it alive for over a century and a half and I am confident it will be alive and well far into the next century.

Sadly, Bill Cook passed from this life April 15, 2011, and although he is no longer here to see the fruits of his many labors, he saw them long before any of the rest of us did.

Yes, Mr. Cook, in answer to your question, these people will stay, people like Sam Townsley, Frank McDonald, Harold McDonald, and Don Anderson, who built their lives around serving this wonderful resort. And the hundreds of people who are now working to bring recreation and relaxation to our guests, they too will stay. And don't worry, future generations who feel a calling to serve in the hospitality field are waiting in the wings to make their appearance; caring, talented young men and women will keep this resort alive and well, for I firmly believe that the French Lick Springs Hotel is as lasting as the hills that surrounds it.

Author Biography

Eva Sharron Kobee spent her childhood in the shadow of the French Lick Springs Hotel where her father, Frank McDonald, worked for 60 years, most of those years as Chief Engineer of the hotel's power plant. While attending Indiana University as a music education major, she worked the summers at the hotel and there met her future husband, Johnny Kobee, a musician in the hotel's band. That summer love turned into a marriage that lasted 57 years and has been blessed with three children, eight grandchildren and nine great-grandchildren....so far. In 2002, while working as the hotel's concierge and historian, she was awarded the Lieutenant Governor's Hoosier Hospitality Award for Orange County. She now lives in Antwerp, Ohio, with her best friend and confidant, "Lady", whom the angels dropped off at the local shelter. Both are proving that you can, indeed, "teach an old dog new tricks".